101
GOLDEN RULES
of
GOLF

1 3 5 7 9 10 8 6 4 2

Published in 2008 by Ebury Press, an imprint of Ebury Publishing

A Random House Group Company

Copyright © 2008 Quid Publishing

The Random House Group Limited Reg. No. 954009

Addresses for companies within the Random House Group can be found at
www.randomhouse.co.uk

A CIP catalogue record for this book is available from the British Library

The Random House Group Limited supports The Forest Stewardship Council (FSC), the leading international forest certification organisation. All our titles that are printed on Greenpeace approved FSC certified paper carry the FSC logo. Our paper procurement policy can be found at www.rbooks.co.uk/environment

To buy books by your favourite authors and register for offers visit www.rbooks.co.uk

Conceived, designed and produced by
Quid Publishing
Level 4 Sheridan House
114 Western Road
Hove BN3 1DD
England
www.quidpublishing.com

Illustrations: Matt Pagett and Steven Bannister
Design: Ali Walper and Lindsey Johns
Printed and bound in China by Midas Printing International

ISBN-13: 978-0-09-192723-3

NOTE
Every effort has been made to ensure that all information contained in this book is correct and compatible with national standards at the time of publication. This book is not intended to replace manufacturers' instructions in the use of their products – always follow their safety guidelines. The author, publisher and copyright holder assume no responsibility for any injury, loss or damage caused or sustained as a consequence of the use and application of the contents of this book.

101
GOLDEN RULES
of
GOLF

WILES, WIT AND
WISDOM TO INFORM
AND ENTERTAIN

Tony Dear

EBURY
PRESS

CONTENTS

Find the grip that feels
most comfortable
to you — see
page 19

Introduction   6

Golf: What's the Point?   8
The Big Dog   10
Loft   11
The Science of Irons   12
Wedges   14
The Perfect Putter   15
The Little White Ball   16
The Grip   18
Gripping Advice   19
Lining It All Up   20
Perfect Posture   21
Ball Position   22
Sport, Game, or Just
a Good Walk Spoiled?   23
Hybrids   24
1st Tee Nerves   25
The Swing   26
The Ball in Flight   28
The Importance of Strategy   30
At a Stretch   32
Bags, Shoes and Gloves   34
Warming Up Right   36

Go Easy on Your Greenkeeper   37
Picking a Pro   38
The Fundamentals of Putting   40
Hit Down to Hit Up   41
What to Wear   42
On the Slopes   44
Heroes   45
Uniqueness   45
Play a Links   46
Hole-in-One   48
Watch Tiger Woods   50
Making Lists   51
Dawn or Dusk?   51
Celebrating the Right Way   52
The Basic Pitch   53
Reading the Greens   54
Masters Tickets   56
Sunscreen   57
The Driving Range   58
The Drinks Cart   59
How to Watch a
Tournament on TV   59
Dealing with a Slice   60
Practice Makes Birdie Putts   62

The Little White Ball
— see page 16

Mastering the Chip 64
Smell the Flowers
(Just Do It Quickly) 65
Beating the Bunkers 66
The Club Pro 68
Crazy Golf 69
The 19th Hole 69
The Good Putter 70
The Dark Art of Gamesmanship 71
The Shank 72
Taking a Decent Photo 73
Making the Ball Bite 74
Thank You... 75
Launch It 76
You are What You Eat 77
A Round With Dad 78
How to Hit the Lob Shot 80
Magnificent Municipals 81
How Green are the Greens? 82
The Golfing Gods 83
Golfers of the World Unite 83
Get Yourself Fitted 84
Keeping Score 86
Go Back and Start Younger 87
A Day at the Open 88
The Rules of the Game 89
Playing With the Pros 90
Playing With the Boss 91
How to Curve
the Ball... Intentionally 92
Your Pre-Shot Routine 94
Etiquette 95
Eye-Balling 96
Hats Off 97
The Yips and
How to Shake Them 98

The Thrill of Matchplay 99
Playing in the Wind 100
Getting a Grip 102
Texas Scramble 103
Where to Buy Your Kit 104
Walk if You Can 105
The Wet Stuff 106
Take It to the Course 107
T-Squares and Weighted Clubs 108
The Irritating Golfer 109
Books 110
On Tees 111
Doing It at Home 112
The Unhelpful Lesson 114
Going Off Piste 115
The Golf Trip 116
Handicaps 118
The Art of Giving 119
Carrying the Bags 120
Golfing for Couples 121
It's All in Your Mind 122
Relax, Easy, Smooth... or Not? 123
The Home of Golf 124
Changes I'd Like to See 125

Index 126

INTRODUCTION

Oh happy days, a golf book. Like the world needs yet another one of these. At my local book shop, there are a couple of long aisles devoted to 'Sport' (or rather 'Sports' because I now live in the States), and a couple more just for golf. There are more books about golf in fact than there are on baseball, basketball and American football combined.

On a recent trip back home to the UK, I noticed that, here too, the golf section in most high-street book stores was sufficiently large to have broken away from the wider 'Sport' shelves. I suppose anything's possible in today's world; but I still couldn't help being surprised by the sight of golf books outnumbering football ones. I guess that this means there is still a huge appetite not just for the game of golf, but also for everything written about it – which can only be a good thing for its future. So, to add to that vast array of golfing literature, here are some of my own thoughts on the game, some the product of idle musings, others the result of hours of painstaking research, I hope you enjoy them all.

IT'S ALL GOOD

101 Golden Rules of Golf is the second in a series of books that seek to inform and entertain. In his introduction to the first – *101 Golden Rules of Fishing* – author Rob Beattie insists that the book is not a 'how to' volume. Sure, there are plenty of tips and useful instruction, but the underlying message is that throwing a hook into a body of water is a fun, gratifying and ultimately fulfilling activity regardless of how many fish end up on that hook. Some of his best trips, he insists, didn't necessarily result in landing a fish. It was the time spent away from the real world, alone or in the company of friends that mattered most, not the number of perch, bass or trout in his net.

The aim of this book is similar. Sure, a round full of triple-bogeys will certainly be every bit as frustrating as an empty net, but I hope even after a round of 121 you can still take some positives home with you, such as the fact you got a bit of sun and holed a putt to break 122.

Even though none of us may amount to anything much on the golf course, I think golfers who learn to appreciate their surroundings, the fresh air, the exercise and banter, who recognize that

The joy that comes from holing a putt to beat 100 for the first time is like no other.

their level of proficiency has no bearing on their worth as a human being and don't take the game too seriously (if you play golf for a living, then go right ahead and curse your bad luck and stress over short putts) can claim to have golf sussed. They may have never shot a course record between them, but they had as much fun as the guy who did.

Well, that's a nice idea, but who am I kidding? Once golf bites, the game frequently becomes an all-consuming burden rather than the harmless pursuit it should be. I know a dozen people for whom golf is a millstone around their neck. The joy they once felt playing the game has all but disappeared.

Fortunately, with the help of work, two kids and a new-found interest in hiking, I have managed to control my own addiction in recent years, though I remember well the days when golf was the point at which life began and ended. Partly through my imitation of that notorious grinder Nick Faldo, and partly because I was a moody teenager, I used to zero in on my target and virtually forget the people with whom I was paired. The really sad part about this is that although I was quite good for a while I was never good enough to justify blanking my playing partners. But then, how good do you have to be to justify ignoring your playing partners? I'm pretty sure the level at which it's okay to be rude doesn't exist.

The great Bobby Jones once said there's golf and then there's tournament golf. I understand what he was getting

A game of golf is a great opportunity to get out in the sunshine, meet new people with a similar passion and wear bad shorts.

at, but ultimately both are supposed to be fun. And if you happen to bank a massive cheque playing the second, then good for you, and it's your turn to get the drinks in.

OUR ROUND

Should we ever be paired together, by all means do whatever you can within the rules to shoot your best score. But for heaven's sake, let's try to make the most of our time away from the real world. I hope you like to talk, laugh and, if it's a social game, play ready golf. Please don't waste time pacing off the yardage or reading your putt from every angle. Leave all that stuff to the pros. And let's judge the success of our round not by how many over or under par we finish but by how keen we are to do it all again.

GOLF: WHAT'S THE POINT?

It's easy to ridicule golf, and golfers; it really is terribly simple to poke fun at us and our game. Consider the fact that until recently our choice of wardrobe made us look truly ludicrous, and we spend thousands on equipment that's unlikely to make much difference and which could be better spent on, oh I don't know, a hundred and one more useful things.

We go out in the snow, talk about the game as if it's the most important thing in the world, and participate with the sort of passion and vigour that our family, friends and careers would surely benefit from. Our shelves droop under the weight of hundreds of 'must read' volumes, most of which we never read. And, at the root of it all, the fact remains that instead of dreaming up plans to make the world a better place we are consumed with thoughts of our next round and how we're going to hit a little white ball around a big field into a small hole.

Of course, when it's put like that the game seems incredibly trivial. Using a similar rationale, one could make any sport or game sound totally inconsequential. No normal person would miss snooker, darts, tennis or fishing, for instance, if they suddenly disappeared. Take away the fact it gives hundreds of millions of people from every part of society and every corner of the planet (apart from America) something to get excited about every weekend and you could even say the same of football; it's just a bunch of kids kicking a ball into a net. Big deal.

REASONS FOR OUR MADNESS

Tragically, many unfortunate people never get further than the cover and therefore fail to discover the worlds we golfers, anglers, footballers and even fans of squash inhabit; but the fact that we golfers are so consumed by our sport can undoubtedly be a good thing. The golf course is an appropriate place to release stress (just don't release it in the direction of your playing partners). Eighteen holes provide a good opportunity for calm, coherent thought. And no one can deny the benefits of walking five miles, socializing with friends, satisfying our need for competition, or simply having an interest that maybe no one else in the family truly understands.

BIG BUSINESS

In addition to that, golf's impact on the economy is immense. In 2005, America's golf-related revenue was $76 billion, making it bigger than the movie industry. Directly and indirectly, it creates roughly two million jobs in the States, and while I don't have the figures for the rest of the world, I do know golf does many economies no harm whatsoever.

It also teaches kids, and a fair few adults besides, the value of sportsmanship, integrity, honesty, companionship and all the other ideals that banal politicians persistently bring up, but which I certainly hope the game instils in my kids.

THE BOTTOM LINE

I suppose the biggest justification for playing golf, however, is that it's just plain fun.

Snow, rain, wind, heat. We don't care.

Some 18 years ago, my mates and I played our own US Masters – not the United States Masters you understand, but the Utterly S**t Masters. The venue was Hollingbury Park in Brighton, England, and a privileged field of ten was invited to compete for the coveted brown jacket I had picked up at a charity shop. (The Masters' version is green, of course, but we thought brown more appropriate.) The runner-up, meanwhile, would become the proud owner of an old, crooked tankard from the same charity shop, bearing the inscription 'For Frank and Betty on their 40th Wedding Anniversary'.

The weather on the day of the tournament was glorious, and with the sun slowly disappearing everyone that had already finished ringed the 18th green as the final group putted out. After Joe, cigarette dangling from his lips and thick, Cossack military trench-coat buttoned all the way from his shins to his neck, holed the last putt of the day we retired to the Half Moon which, as luck would have it, was owned by the winner's dad.

Over beer and sandwiches, we awarded the jacket and agreed this should become an annual event (alas, university, weddings, babies and jobs have all decided otherwise). By the end of the evening, somewhat the worse for wear, we were raising a glass to the canny Scotsmen who invented the game – I'll never forget it.

⚘ THE BIG DOG

Golf club manufacturers aren't stupid. They know how pumped up we get from smashing a big, looping drive straight past our pals' balls. Consequently, they invest millions and millions of dollars into producing ever larger, shinier, more powerful drivers to satisfy the caveman in every golfer.

Twenty years ago, drivers were more or less judged by looks alone. Persimmon woods were very beautiful – lovingly carved, shaped, whipped and varnished – but beyond their appearance there wasn't much to get excited about. I had a persimmon Mizuno driver that was so attractive I didn't want to ever chip or scratch it by hitting a golf ball, so I kept it hidden in the garage, bringing it out only on very special occasions. It was very nice to look at and all, but so technologically inferior to modern drivers that an annotated drawing would have had just one line, pointing to the clubhead, with the caption, 'Nice-looking clubhead'. My, how times change.

SPACE-AGE DRIVERS

These days, annotated diagrams of drivers look like a map of the London Underground. The most popular driver on the market not only boasts an all-titanium deep-face head, but four little screws (two 14g weights, two 1g weights) that can be moved around four different holes in the sole of the club to promote certain types of shots – more weight near the heel (nearer the shaft) for a draw, more near the toe for a fade. It has Inverted Cone Technology (this business of referring to even the smallest innovation as 'Such and Such' technology is very tedious), a very low

Centre of Gravity, enhanced gear effect and, get this, an eMOI of 5800.

'An eMOI of 5800!' I hear you gasp. 'They can't be serious.'

Knowing what an eMOI is, and whether or not one of 5800 is better than one of 6000, really doesn't matter, of course. What does is that the combination of space-age materials and technical expertise behind these new clubs enables you to smack your golf ball further than you ever did in the dark ages. Major developments to the ball (see page 16) and, to a lesser degree, the shaft (see page 85) in your club make significant contributions to longer drives, but the driver now looks so sleek and dangerous we assume it must be all the driver head's doing. The gold, red, blue, green, or yellow graphite shaft in your driver does at least look somewhat more hi-tech than the simple steel rod of yesteryear, but your ball is still round and white with little dimples on it.

Your driver head has changed almost beyond recognition, especially if you purchased one of those square-headed Nike or Callaway clubs, which promised to hit the ball straighter than anything had before, and probably did.

Even a club as advanced as the r7 Superquad may be obsolete by the time this book is published.

LOFT

It's no good having all this technology at your disposal if you purchase the wrong club, and by the wrong club I mean one with insufficient loft. A few years back, one of the ways men compared their masculinity against that of other men was by comparing driver lofts — the lower the better.

So, a guy with a 7° club was quite a bit manlier (he probably earned more, could bench press more and was certainly better in bed) than a guy with an 11° driver. The thinking was that the wimp who needed 11° of loft was so puny he couldn't get the ball up in the air without a good deal of help from his equipment, whereas the guy with just 7° was so big and powerful and created so much clubhead speed that he had a hard time keeping his ball below outer space.

What happened, of course, was that anyone with a 7° driver who wasn't a regular winner on one of the professional golf tours or in the major championships spent years pounding his ball into the ground, at least never hitting it above knee height (I probably did this for five years before seeing the light), and playing his next shot from a good distance behind the 11° guy. 'Didn't quite get that one,' we'd say. 'But when I do, watch out.'

At the turn of the century, research found that, because of the way the ball was developing, everyone besides a few genuine bombers like Tiger Woods and John Daly needed more loft if they wanted to maximize the distance they hit the ball.

The average golfer with a swingspeed of 90mph (145 kmph) needs a driver with a good 11°, maybe 12°, of loft. Anything less and you probably aren't hitting your tees shots as far as you could. Friends who did go to the trouble of getting the most suitable driver for their swing and swingspeed may now be busting it past you, making golf considerably less fun than it should be.

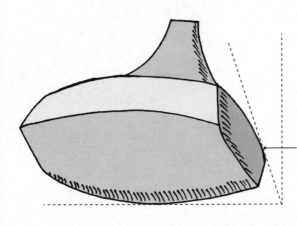

Always use a driver with the right amount of loft for your swingspeed and angle of attack. A typical 15–18 handicapper should have at least 10°, or even as much as 12°.

A clubhead's loft is the angle at which the face is set back from vertical.

THE SCIENCE OF IRONS

Iron clubheads may not have seen quite as many changes as drivers or putters in recent years — they're still the same basic shape and size — but they haven't exactly stood still either. Thinner faces, alloy face inserts, heel/toe tungsten inserts, urethane cavity inserts and wider soles have all made modern irons so much easier to hit than what granddad used.

Keeping abreast of new iron launches ten years back wasn't difficult. The manufacturers realized that distance was the be-all-and-end-all for most golfers so most of their R&D budgets were ploughed into drivers and balls. Now you just need to blink a couple of times and TaylorMade, Callaway or Mizuno have changed their entire iron inventory. It really doesn't take long for any club, irons included, to start looking a bit dated.

CAVITY-BACKS OR MUSCLE-BACKS?
Until 1961 when Ping introduced the first perimeter-weighted irons, clubheads were very basic-looking chunks of metal only slightly wider in the sole than at the top and possessing absolutely no game-improvement features whatsoever. They were so unforgiving that if you thinned a shot on a cold, frosty morning, you would still be feeling the rattle in your hands and arms four holes later.

Thankfully, other manufacturers, following Ping's lead, soon started moving the club's weight from the middle to the outside of the head, thus increasing its resistance to twist following off-centre strikes. The game became an awful lot easier as a result because badly struck shots were now ending up somewhere near the green instead of squirting off sideways into the bushes.

Cavity-backs have come a long way since those early days and now have so many bells and whistles it's a wonder they don't swing themselves. Just check out what TaylorMade's r7 CGB has going on: a thin 17-4 stainless steel face; 'Distance-Enhancing Inverted Cone Technology' (the inverted cone is milled directly onto the inner side of the clubface and increases ball velocity); a hollow top-line that allows discretionary weight to be placed more effectively around the clubhead's perimeter; and toe/heel tungsten weights that further enhance the club's stability. Basically, if you can't hit a ball high, far and straight with one of these you must be useless.

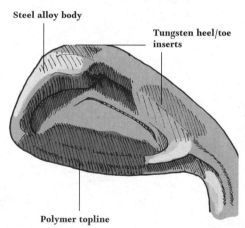

Steel alloy body

Tungsten heel/toe inserts

Polymer topline

Granddad wouldn't recognize a modern cavity-back iron like the TaylorMade r7 CGB or Cobra VF1 (above).

Not surprisingly, cavity-backs account for well over 80 per cent of iron sales and I'm telling you here and now to buy them. They are available at virtually all price points so you will have no bother finding the right set for you.

The alternative is the blade, which has progressed significantly from the days when you could shave or cut bread with it, but which remains the domain of highly skilled golfers (bear in mind though that far more pros use cavity backs than blades). Blades have come on so much, in fact, they even go by a new name – muscle-backs – but they're still the callous, ruthless, pitiless clubs they always were; only slightly more tolerant of your imperfect strikes than they were years ago.

So why would anyone use them? Because good players are able to shape shots better, and when you do catch it flush there might not be a better feeling in the universe.

CAST OR FORGED

The vast majority (but not all) of cavity-back heads are made using the investment-cast process in which molten metal (usually stainless steel with a little chromium and nickel) is poured into clubhead-shaped ceramic/sand moulds, then cooled. Blades/muscle-backs are forged (again, not all of them) from softer carbon steel in a manner not too dissimilar to how the village blacksmith used to work, the difference being that forged golf clubs are now squeezed into shape by a highly technical machine called a press rather than hammered into submission on the anvil.

Forged clubheads are supposed to feel a bit softer than cast heads and there's still a market for them despite the fact various studies have shown few golfers, not even tour pros, can feel the difference. Unless, that is, in their wallet – as they are quite a bit more expensive too.

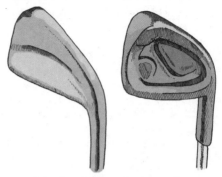

A muscle-back and a cavity-back iron. The one on the right is for you and me. The one on the left is for Tiger and his pals on the pro tours.

Your set

Most sets come with eights irons – from a 3-iron with about 20° of loft, to a pitching wedge with 48° – although some manufacturers, most notably Adams, don't bother with 3-, 4-, and sometimes even 5-irons, replacing them with hybrid clubs (see page 24) that are considerably easier to get off the ground and high in the air than standard long irons. I would recommend anyone with a handicap of, say, 12 and above seriously considering this hybrid/iron mix. After all, why bother buying long irons that you're never going to use; or, if you do use them, will land you in trouble?

⚜ WEDGES

Necessity is the mother of invention so it was inevitable the old pitching wedge–sand wedge combo would one day be updated. The gap between the typical 48° pitching wedge and 56° sand wedge needed filling, and 56° wasn't quite enough loft for an almost vertical lob shot that lands on the green like a balloon.

So the 52° gap or approach wedge and 60° lob wedge were born and suddenly golfers were hitting a vast array of short-game shorts they hadn't been able to before without manipulating the clubhead somehow.

This standard four-wedge set soon became obsolete itself though with extra lofts, bounce angles and finishes (chrome, rust, beryllium copper, black, gun-metal, oil can, satin) being added all the time. The result is a staggering choice of wedges, apt really to make a right-side-of-the-brain dreamer like myself a bit confused. And they don't even have names any more – often, wedges are simply known by their lofts.

How Many Should You Have?

I've survived with three – a 48° pitching wedge with 8° of bounce, a 56° sand wedge with 12° of bounce and a 60° lob wedge with 6° of bounce – for years without ever really thinking I could do with an X° wedge with Y° of bounce. I tried a 52°

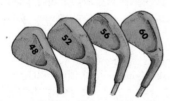

A pro might want all four wedges for specific shots, but the average golfer should get by with lofts of 48° (PW), 56° (SW) and 60° (LW). By not adding a fourth, you can keep a 5-wood or hybrid which you'll find much more useful.

wedge for a while, but found I missed the lofted wood I'd had to forego.

I'm fairly certain that most mid-to-high handicappers could get by with a similar set-up, maybe selecting wedges with more bounce if their course has soft, fluffy sand and moist, lush turf, or less bounce if they play at a links where the lies are much tighter and the bunker sand much firmer.

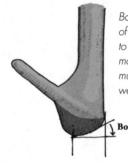

Bounce is the angle of the sole in relation to the ground and it makes bunker shots so much easier than they were back in the day.

Bounce angle

What is Bounce?

In 1931, after taking a flight with Howard Hughes during which Hughes explained that an aeroplane's battle with drag was similar to that of a pitching wedge's with sand, then three-time major champion Gene Sarazen began messing about with his wedge. He soldered metal onto the bottom – making the club's trailing edge rest on the ground with the leading edge raised slightly – to enable the club to splash through the sand rather than dig into it. The metal on the sole gave the club 'bounce', the angle between the sole and the ground. It changed bunker technique forever.

THE PERFECT PUTTER

Your putter sees a lot of action, hitting almost 50 per cent of the shots you ever play. So it makes sense to find one that works and, when you do, to guard it with your life.

Despite the fact so many of their shots are used up on the green, most golfers practise their putting about as frequently as Haley's Comet passes by. And even though improving their putting is just about the easiest way to lower their scores (Jack Nicklaus once said that while few golfers could ever attain his level of ball-striking, anyone could become as good a putter as him), most will splurge thousands on new drivers, irons, shirts, balls and green fees before they spend so much as a penny on a new putter.

Part of the reason as I see it, is that golfers don't want to spend any cash on any item that could be replaced, though not terribly effectively, by an empty coke can tied to the end of a stick. And nor do they feel the need to practise a part of the game that looks so innocuous, is really quite dull and which can't put them in any trees or lakes unless they're really, really bad.

But I think the main reason why the driving range gets busy while the putting green looks on empty, and why golfers don't take the time to get fitted properly for a putter is because they are so darned expensive. I don't know when they became so pricey, but I do know that if I ever found a spare bundle of notes lying about, I wouldn't be spending them on a putter.

We really should be paying more attention to our putting though. There's very little I can tell you about choosing a putter, however, other than to go for whatever you think will help you hole the most putts. It may be short, long, have a face insert or tiny grooves, be centre-shafted or heel-shafted, blade or mallet.

For some reason blade putters are now the type that used to be called heel/toe weighted putters, while genuine blades have all but disappeared. Mallets, on the other hand, used to look like, er, mallets but today put you in mind of Transformers (the hi-tech kids' toy, not the device that transfers electrical energy from one circuit to another through inductively coupled electrical conductors). Which style you choose is all down to personal preference. For the record, I like a nice Ping-Anser-style blade, with a 36in-long shaft and can't abide the wacky, extra-terrestrial mallets. You'd have to pay me to use one of those.

The putter on the left won't eat you, but it might help if you rarely find the middle of the putterface. Many modern blades retain the popular Ping-Anser shape (right) and have sufficient heel/toe weighting to stabilize poor strikes.

THE LITTLE WHITE BALL

The golf ball is in big trouble. It's going too far... for the pros, anyway. These days, great players from the past, most notably Jack Nicklaus and Arnold Palmer, are up in arms about the distance modern tour pros are hitting it. The classic tracks they used to find demanding are now mere pitch-and-putt courses that require no more than a driver, a bunch of wedges and a putter – or so they say.

BETTER BALLS, LONGER HOLES

Tiger Woods went round 72 holes at Hoylake in the 2006 Open Championship hitting his driver only once, and that got him into trouble. The rest of the time he used a 2-iron off the tee, taking advantage of the bone-hard fairways. He won by two with a score of 18 under par. Seems the oldies have a point.

It certainly is the case that without a stout wind or knee-deep rough, Hoylake, the Old Course at St Andrews, Muirfield, Sunningdale, Merion, the National Golf Links and a host of other great courses around the world no longer test the best. So they either stop hosting professional tournaments altogether, or get lengthened, and lengthened, and lengthened...

This is regrettable, certainly. I used to love watching the European Open on the Old Course at Sunningdale in Surrey, but by the mid-1990s the course had become obsolete as a tournament venue. And without crossing the old London Road or stealing a few acres from the adjacent New Course, that's how it's going to stay.

At the same time, if people watch the pros on TV playing 7,500-yard courses, then they demand the same. This is utter madness, of course, as most golfers can't

Does it Really Matter which Ball You Use?

OK, I'm sorry, I'm just ranting now. The point of this page was to give you some hints as to what sort of ball is best for you. Well, let me start by saying that if you can't break 100, it really doesn't matter, so I suggest you stop forking out your hard-earned cash for Pro-V1s and instead buy Top-Flites from the supermarket. With all due respect, you are not hitting it hard enough to gain any advantage from all the hi-tech stuff going on in the modern ball. Only when you start driving it a decent distance and are knocking on 79's door should you concern yourself with what type of ball you're playing and consider using a fancy three- or four-piece ball such as the Pro-V1, HX Tour, or Nike One Platinum. Only at this level will you begin to appreciate the extra distance, stable ball flight, piercing trajectory and responsive feel around the greens that justify these balls' price tags.

break 80, or even 90, from the middle tees, so hitting off the back tees makes scores that are perfectly high enough already, thank you very much, even higher. What's worse is that longer courses require more land, which costs more money, which bumps green fees up. Longer courses also take longer to play, which is part of the reason why many people are leaving the game and why fewer and fewer are choosing to take it up.

IN PRAISE OF BETTER BALLS
Many would argue those are all perfectly sound reasons to stop any further improvements to the ball, or even roll it back a few years. I say, just hold on a minute there, cowboy.

The fact is, handicaps are not coming down. The average golfer had a hard time breaking 100 twenty years ago, and still does, even with the multi-layer, urethane-covered ball. The 6,500-yarder we've been playing for years still provides as much sport as most of us can handle. However, even though our scores aren't coming down, we've become accustomed to hitting our Titleist Pro-V1s and Callaway HX Tours. To go back to a lighter, less aerodynamic ball would be hard to swallow.

So, what do we do? Well, allow me to throw a couple of suggestions out there:

+ Roll the ball back by all means, but only for the fraction of players for whom Merion and Sunningdale, and so on are now too short – in other words, the pros.
+ Keep the ball as it is and cut fairways longer, so shots don't run as far.

What's Inside?

The rise of the solid, multi-layered, urethane-covered ball led to the demise of the wound ball because the former provides a combination of distance, durability and feel that balata balls never could. Today's balls fly on a shallower, more parabolic trajectory than soft-wound balls.

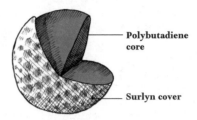

Today's two-piece ball

Polybutadiene core

Surlyn cover

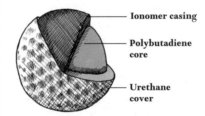

Today's multi-layered ball

Ionomer casing

Polybutadiene core

Urethane cover

+ Make the rough longer so there is actually a penalty for finding it.
+ Stagger fairway bunkers a good distance up the hole so no matter how far you hit it off the tee there's a bunker waiting for you if you stray offline. And make those bunkers deep.

THE GRIP

To play golf at a level where you can score in the 80s, 70s, and maybe even the 60s, you've first got to learn how to hold the club correctly. For the beginner, the recommended grip feels uncomfortable, but a few minutes' practice every day will make it feel natural in no time. I suggest you do it, because without a decent grip you are making an already hard game harder.

As someone who has taught the game for a living, I'm confident I could predict the shape of your shots by observing how you hold the club. Actually, there's a fairly simple formula involved here: a weak grip tends to fade or slice the ball; a strong one draws or hooks it.

WEAK VERSUS STRONG

So what is a weak grip exactly, what is strong, and what's in-between? Contrary to what you might be thinking, a weak grip doesn't mean you're holding the club too lightly and a strong one doesn't mean your hold is too tight.

No, a weak grip is one in which you can see too much of the palm of the top hand, or too much of the back of the bottom hand. Assuming the leading edge of the clubface was perpendicular to the target line as you addressed the ball (and was therefore 'square' to the target), the clubface is more than likely to be open, or facing to the right, when you strike the ball because your forearms will have a hard time rotating properly and bringing the clubface back to square. This imparts left-to-right sidespin on the ball, making it curve to the right. Conversely, a strong grip promotes too much forearm rotation and causes the clubface at impact to be closed, or pointing to the left of your target. And that means a low, slinging hook, probably heading for trouble. For a weak or strong grip to be successful

(and there certainly have been players who have done well with what appear to be poor grips), you must therefore manipulate the forearms and hands in order to hit the ball with a square clubface — hold off the release if you favour a strong grip, or exaggerate it with a weak grip. That is why the great teacher, Harvey Penick said that if you have a bad grip, you need a bad swing to compensate.

Unless you're blessed with the talent of Jose Maria Olazabal (weak), or Fred Couples, Paul Azinger, Bernhard Langer, John Daly and so on (strong), then holding off or exaggerating the release with any degree of consistency just isn't going to happen. Your clubface will rarely be square to the target line and you'll be fighting a hook or a slice all day. And that's no fun.

A neutral grip, neither weak nor strong, is therefore to be encouraged. Just feel like the back of your top hand and palm of the bottom hand face the target. If you want to make your grip slightly stronger, and many people do as it encourages a slight draw and consequently a few more yards, simply turn both hands clockwise slightly (right-handers).

Now, grip the club lightly – about four on a scale of one to ten – in the fingers of each hand rather than across the palms, and smile as your ball flies straight for a change.

CONNECTING THE HANDS

No one ever played good golf with their hands separated on the club. The question is how are you going to bring them together? There are three basic methods, known as: Baseball, Vardon and Interlocking.

✦ Baseball: All ten fingers in contact with the club, but the little finger of the bottom hand presses against the index finger of the top hand.
✦ Vardon (or Overlapping): Named after the great Jersey-born player Harry Vardon who didn't invent it but did make it famous, this grip moves the little finger of the bottom hand so it settles in the groove between the index and middle fingers of the top hand.
✦ Interlocking: Achieved simply by twisting the index finger of the top hand and the little finger of the bottom around each other.

Just go with whichever grip feels most comfortable to you.

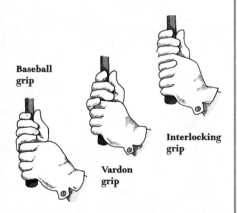

Baseball grip

Vardon grip

Interlocking grip

Gripping Advice

On the Thursday of the 1987 Open Championship at Muirfield in Scotland, well-known teacher John Jacobs was giving a free clinic to members of an awed public in the huge exhibition tent. Jacobs, a genial Yorkshireman credited with improving the games of several great players, was talking about grips and I was leaning on his every word having suspected for a long time that my dodgy hold on the club may have been to blame for years of less than stellar golf.

As he left the stage to much applause, I barged through, desperate to catch him. 'Mr Jacobs, Mr Jacobs, I'm rubbish at golf, can you help?' Okay, those might not have been the actual words, but that's pretty much how I felt. 'Certainly son,' he beamed. 'Show me your grip.' Before I had even put my bottom hand on the club, he said, 'Ah, so you're a slicer.'

His swift analysis and correct assessment (I did indeed suffer from an unholy slice) were stunning. I mean, I was quite literally stunned. How could he possibly know which way my ball flew from the position of my left hand? The man had obviously sold his soul to the devil in return for the knowledge of good and evil, or at least the difference between a good and bad golf grip. 'Just turn your top hand clockwise so the "V" formed between your thumb and index finger points to your right shoulder,' he said. Lesson over. I was drawing the ball within a week.

LINING IT ALL UP

The grip got two pages all to itself and both alignment and posture warrant at least that, if not more; but if you're as hooked on the game as I am, I'm sure you already have a library stacked with books showing you how to stand to the ball. So let's keep it brief...

No doubt about it, most bad shots are caused by errors in the set-up. Jack Nicklaus used to say if you addressed the ball correctly, you were 75 per cent of the way to hitting a good shot, or was it 85 per cent, or 95 per cent... In any case, the point is that only by aligning yourself and the clubface correctly will you hit the ball in the desired direction, and only by adopting the correct posture will you create a solid base, help maintain your balance to the end of the swing and facilitate a wide, smooth swing.

SQUARE

The word 'square' is used so often when talking about body and clubface alignment, it definitely pays to know what it means. Your body is square to the target if your feet, knees, hips and shoulders are aligned parallel left of it, by which I mean if you stand two and a half feet from the ball you should ideally align your body two and a half feet left of the hole (provided the hole is your target of course). Your clubface is square to your body if it points in the same direction, wherever that may be, and it's square to the target if the leading edge is perpendicular (at right angles) to an imaginary line linking the two.

If all that sounds a trifle complex, it can be summed up simply by imagining you're standing on the inner rail of a train track with the ball on the outer rail. The target is at a point in the distance on the outer rail.

Doesn't that make it all a lot easier to understand? For a straight shot your body is aligned straight down the inner rail while the clubface points at the target on the outer rail. If you wanted to fade the ball (left to right), you'd start by bringing your left foot and left side away from the rail slightly, thus aligning your feet and shoulders to the left of the target (see page 93). To hit a draw, you'd align your feet and shoulders across the tracks (see page 92). The clubface, however, remains pointed at the target in both instances.

If your body is aligned square to the target and you want your clubface to be square as well and therefore hit a straight shot at the target (never a bad option), this is what it should look like.

PERFECT POSTURE

Watch all the great players and you won't see two swings alike. But rewind the tape, look a little closer and you'll notice they all start from a fairly similar position. Yes, some players appear slightly taller and more erect than others, while some may look a little stiffer, but, with very few exceptions, professionals get the various elements of their posture right.

There are more elaborate, scientific-sounding procedures for guaranteeing you stand to the ball correctly, but I think it can be summed up with the following: knees flexed; bum out; back straight; chin up. Your feet should be slightly wider than shoulder-width apart when hitting a driver, and inch closer together as the club gets shorter.

Develop good posture and you won't look unlike a goalkeeper getting ready to save a penalty, though he may have a little more flex in the knees than you require. What is more, not only will you strike the ball better, but you're unlikely to suffer as many back complaints as golfers whose posture is faulty.

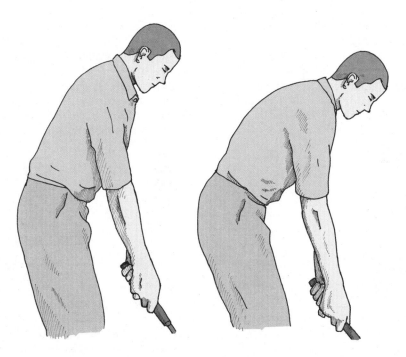

The golfer on the left looks relaxed but athletic, he is primed ready to fire. The golfer on the right is slouching, has a rounded back and is not in a good position to make a balanced and powerful swing.

BALL POSITION

Positioning the ball incorrectly a fraction either side of where it should be could mean the difference between the lake and a very makeable putt for birdie. It's difficult and probably futile ranking the different parts of your set-up in order of importance, but many teachers consider the importance of ball position second only to the grip.

Position the ball correctly and your clubhead will approach impact at an appropriate angle of descent, reach the bottom of its arc a split second after making contact (taking a shallow divot, squeezing the ball off the turf and creating a little backspin) and hit the ball squarely. Put it too far forward, however, and your shoulders will be open to your target (aligned to the left) and the clubhead will have started moving inside the target line when it contacts the ball which will almost certainly start left. The club will also have bottomed out already so you may hit it fat too. That's a lot of things going wrong! Likewise, if it's too far back in your stance, your shoulders will be slightly closed (aligned right) and a push, or block, becomes likely.

DIFFERENT THEORIES

For 20 years I, like most golfers, positioned the ball in relation to my feet. But I recently came across what might be a better method for guaranteeing the right position; playing it opposite various points on my left side. (Not having known about this until now clearly explains why I never won the Open.) This makes sense because the person who pushes his or her feet unnaturally far apart (I've seen guys with legs spread so wide a fat pig could get through) and plays the ball off the left heel will probably start with their

Driver – Opposite the outside of your left shoulder (which for most people is about the same place as the inside of the front foot).

Fairway wood or hybrid off the ground – Opposite your left armpit (about two inches behind where it was for the driver).

Long and medium irons – Opposite your left ear (two inches further back still).

Short irons or wedges – Opposite your left cheek (just forward of centre).

hands too far behind the ball. And that doesn't work.

Most golfers agree the ball should come back as the club gets shorter, but while many think it should move back half an inch or so for every club until it reaches the middle of the stance with the 9-iron or pitching wedge, others prefer playing all their iron shots with the ball very slightly forward of centre. That doesn't work for me because it creates slightly too steep an attack with the long irons.

And then there's nine-time major champion Ben Hogan who played the ball an inch or so inside his left heel for every shot he played. It was just his right foot that moved – closer to the left, and across the line (see below), as the club got shorter.

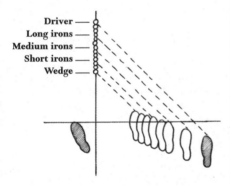

You'll notice Hogan's stance was closed for the woods and long irons in relation to his target. He did this because it helped establish an image of the preferred path of the clubhead – approaching the ball from the inside – and to clear the right side of his body in the backswing. The only time his stance was perfectly square was with the mid-irons. With the short irons he opened his stance to promote a high, accurate fade that stopped quickly after pitching.

GOLFING MATTERS

Sport, Game, or Just a Good Walk Spoiled?

Mark Twain obviously never felt the thrill of coming up the 18th needing a par to win. He never hit a perfect drive high against a perfect blue sky that stayed in the air seemingly forever and dropped to Earth 280 yards ahead of him. And he never played a British links course on a summer's day and finished as a huge, red sun finally dipped below the horizon. If he had, he would never have uttered such tosh – a good walk spoiled, indeed. We'll reject Twain's musings, but the question of golf being a sport or game remains.

Thirty years ago, before Tiger Woods came along, and when a number of players actually hit shots while taking a drag on a cigar or cigarette, few would have regarded it as sport, a good smoke spoiled maybe.

In the modern age, however, following the example set by Woods, players are building Popeye forearms and bionic legs. They're working out several times a week to build the stamina they need to survive three practice rounds, four tournament rounds, the crush of media requests and countless international corporate outings. Of course it's a sport. And if you ever saw Seve Ballesteros or Lee Trevino play, you'd say it was an art too.

HYBRIDS

Nothing says equipment boom or helps out high-handicap golfers quite like the hybrid. The driver has certainly had its share of attention in the last decade, and some putters now have what look like claws or fangs sticking out their backs. But improvements to these clubs make existing shots slightly easier. A hybrid is so versatile and so easy to hit, it gives you shots you never had before.

Call me strange, but the shot that always used to instil fear in me wasn't escaping a greenside bunker from a plugged lie, the fairway bunker shot, the lob shot to a tight pin, the drive to a precariously narrow fairway, or even the tee shot over water; no, it was a 3-wood off the turf.

And I'm not talking about a 3-wood off a significant slope, or into a strong wind, merely a straightforward shot of 210–220 yards say, off a perfectly level lie with no wind, water or woodpeckers to upset me.

But no more do I dread this distance, or lay up with a 6-iron and wedge on – pretty low I know, but if you saw some of my 3-wood shots… Now I just uncork my 18° hybrid, make a nice easy swing and watch the ball fly high, land soft and cosy up to the hole. Well, to be honest that's only happened about four times, but that is four times more than it ever happened with a 3-wood.

WHAT'S A HYBRID?

A hybrid looks like a small-headed wood, but plays as easily as a mid-iron thanks to the position of the centre of gravity (CG). Because of a hybrid's dimensions, the CG is positioned much lower and further back in the head than in long irons which results in a much higher trajectory than a shot played

The first time I saw someone chip with a hybrid I did a double-take. The first time I tried it, I too became a believer.

with an iron of the same loft. So you can hit a 210–220 yard shot with a club that's as easy to hit and which produces the same sort of trajectory as a 5-iron. It's great out of the rough and you can chip with it too.

Hybrid – Long-Iron Equivalents

A 17° hybrid has roughly the same loft as a 2-iron, while a 20° hybrid is the equivalent of a 3-iron.
23° – 4-iron
26° – 5-iron
29° – 6-iron
32° – 7-iron

NB These are the figures for Callaway's Big Bertha Heavenwood Hybrids and may not be the same as other manufacturers' clubs. Adams' IDEA Pro, for instance, comes in five lofts: 16°, 18°, 20°, 23° and 26°.

It looks like a small wood but plays like a 5-iron. Give the person who came up with that concept a medal.

1ST TEE NERVES

Unless they're coming down the stretch knowing they have a chance to take home a pro-shop gift certificate for winning the monthly medal, there is nowhere amateur golfers are more jittery than on the 1st tee.

I'll never forget the day my mate John succumbed to nerves on the opening hole at Southport and Ainsdale GC in Lancashire. He'll forgive me for saying this, but John is not Ryder Cup material. So it's not surprising that, as he stood on the tee of this intimidating 204-yard par 3, called 'Trial', with the wind blowing in his face and four elderly members looking on, he became more than a little self-conscious.

He shouldn't have done it, but John interrupted his pre-shot routine to take one last look at the small, but intimidating, gallery assembled behind him. He addressed his ball thinking only of how he could avoid embarrassing himself. Clearly, he was not 'in the zone'.

John's swing is fairly quick at the best of times, but on this occasion it was barely perceptible. The foot long, six-inch deep divot he carved out of the ground definitely was though. Thanks to the size of this great clod of earth, John's clubhead was barely moving by the time it reached the ball which barely toppled off the tee. His face a swelling purple, John turned to me for direction, clearly at a loss over what to do. In the end, I think he just pocketed his ball, told me to meet him on the 2nd tee and ran off.

OVERCOMING FEAR

John's primary emotion as he lined up to hit was fear. All he could think about were the distinguished gentlemen lining the tee, and what they might do should he duff it. When you're playing your best

you forget about who's watching, swing mechanics and what the consequences might be – you are absorbed by the process rather than overcome with fear.

John needed to take a few deep breaths and focus on slowing his heartbeat. At the same time, he should have been visualizing exactly where he wanted his ball to go, and then gone through his pre-shot routine (see page 94) without ever losing the mental image of a successful outcome. Of course, he didn't want to spend two or three minutes doing all that, but nor did he want to stand over the ball wondering just how bad his shot might turn out.

Probably easier said than done, but just block the people watching out of your mind. And really, in the big scheme of things, who cares about your shot? It matters not one bit if you make a hole-in-one or hit it backwards. Just hit it and go find it.

⚒ THE SWING

In March 1916, Ernest Jones was badly injured in a battle with German artillery near Loos in France. He had 16 pieces of metal removed from his head, right forearm and right leg, which was subsequently amputated below the knee. Four months later, walking with the aid of an artificial limb, he shot 83 at Royal Norwich in Norfolk, England. A few weeks after that he had a 72 at Clacton in Essex.

That Ernest Jones should overcome such an obvious and restricting disability as this to shoot the scores he did and later become one of the best teachers of his day (and perhaps in the history of the game) suggests that more than anyone perhaps, Jones understood the secret to good golf. So what was his secret? Swing the clubhead.

Yes indeed, swing the clubhead. Don't go looking for variations, explanations, elaborations, or additions. Letting the clubhead swing, you see, creates far more centrifugal force (and consequently distance) than you'll ever get with a series of technically correct but swingspeed-sapping positions that you piece together.

The perfect golf swing should not feel like a series of set positions, but one continuous, flowing motion. It's the only way you'll ever generate clubhead speed.

TEACHING THE SWING

Today's teachers don't dismiss tempo and centrifugal force altogether, but they seem far more concerned with angles and the positions of the clubhead and body before and during the swing. With all due respect, these teachers have to pay the staff they employ at their numerous 'academies' around the world somehow and they aren't going to do that by issuing one simple three-word instruction to every player they meet. People might catch on, after all.

Of course, you also need to be holding the club correctly, exhibiting sound posture, and have the ball positioned between your feet in just the right spot to hit the ball sweetly, and it would be wrong to suggest stockpiles of instruction books, magazine articles, videos, DVDs, downloads and so on actually make the average Joe worse at golf than he otherwise could be. But for

most normal people (people with jobs, kids and insufficient free time in which to practise eight hours a day), too much knowledge can be a bad thing.

FORCE VERSUS POWER

Jones emphasized the application of force over power. Everyone has power, he said, some more than others, but not everyone can apply that power correctly to a stationary golf ball. If they could, Phil Pfister of Charleston, West Virginia, currently the world's strongest man, would be the best golfer in the world, or at least the longest hitter of a golf ball. He's neither.

Jones asserted the only way to ensure all your power is directed forcefully into the back of the ball at the exact moment of impact is by forgetting mechanics, swinging the clubhead, and allowing the wrists, elbows, shoulders, hips, legs, knees, ankles and toes to move naturally as they do when you are walking, and for them to follow the lead of the hands. 'All other motions are admirable as followers,' he said, 'but disastrous as leaders.'

Jones was constantly asked by people he met what the problem with their swing was. 'Nothing,' he would reply. 'You do not have a swing.'

Keep it Simple

I'll bet there are times when you do swing the club beautifully, gracefully even. When? Immediately after having sliced one into the trees. You storm over to your bag, pick out another ball, tee it up and hit it without a single thought as to how you're doing it. Beginners first need to familiarize themselves with the correct grip, posture and ball position. But players who have been playing a while and have all that stuff down need to forget about swing planes, supernating wrists and the like, and just swing their clubhead.

THE BALL IN FLIGHT

John Jacobs was the first teacher to discuss ball flight laws – why the ball behaves the way it does – in any great depth, back in the early '70s. His theories went largely uncontested until the turn of this century when science and technology had to stick their oar in and muddy the waters.

Type 'golf shot's initial direction' into any search engine and you will get a plethora of matches. Inevitably, on the first few pages of results you find several sites that agree unreservedly with what Jacob's called 'golf's geometry'. In his book *Practical Golf*, Jacobs discussed 'golf's four vital impact elements' – clubhead path, clubface angle, angle of descent and clubhead speed – at great length, concluding, among other things, that the path of your clubhead dictates the direction in which your ball starts. Subsequent curvature – hooking to the left or slicing to the right – is caused, he added, by the angle of the clubface at impact in relation to its path.

Jacobs taught that a straight pull to the left is caused by an out-to-in swingpath with the clubface square to that path (in other words closed to the target). A pull-hook (starts left, curves further left) occurs when the clubface is closed in relation to the out-to-in path and a pull-slice (starts left, slices right) is the result of a face that is open to that clubhead path.

Knowing all this made it easy to work out why a block-push (straight right), hook (starts right, curves way left) or push-slice (starts right, goes further right) happens. And it also allowed me to decipher how I hit the ball straight at my target, or why it might curve left or right after starting out on the intended line. I learned this lesson young, have lived by it since, and even taught it to others.

JACOBS' CHALLENGERS

Unfortunately, as is so often the case, that's not quite the whole truth, and a handful of the results for that web search we carried out earlier will take you to sites that refute Jacobs' theories. One of them even goes as far as to call his ball flight laws the 'Ball Flight Lies'.

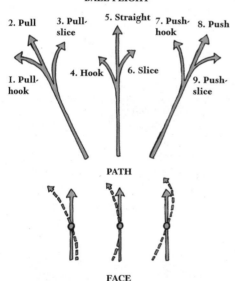

BALL FLIGHT

2. Pull   3. Pull-slice   5. Straight   7. Push-hook   8. Push

1. Pull-hook   4. Hook   6. Slice   9. Push-slice

PATH

FACE

Closed ➤ Pull-hook   Hook   Push-hook
Square ➤ Pull   Straight   Push
Open ➤ Pull-slice   Slice   Push-slice

I've hit every one of these shots several thousand times each. It definitely pays to know how swingpath and face angle affect a shot.

The authors of these sites insist that the clubface angle has a far greater effect on initial direction than its path, saying the ball starts on a line more or less perpendicular to the clubface regardless of its path. Your clubhead may be moving from out-to-in, they say, but the ball can still start true.

WHO'S RIGHT?

I've done more than enough research to tell you I haven't really got a clue. But after 20 years of hitting every kind of shot under the sun, and testing it out on the range countless times by hitting intentional hooks, slices, pulls and blocks, I'm sticking with Jacobs. And Jack Nicklaus is a firm believer too, at least he was when he wrote the following in 2001: 'The out-to-in path produces pulled shots when the clubface alignment matches it, or a left-to-right slice when the clubface is open to it at impact.' Seems pretty unambiguous to me.

Also, I'm not sure I understand how the clubface theory explains how a ball could start left and slice back to the centre – a very common shot. Your ball starts left of the target if the face is closed at impact, they say; but if the face is closed, and slice spin is caused by an open face, how does the ball slice back? Perhaps I'm missing something here.

However, because this theory has numerous backers who I assume are challenging Jacobs' assertions based on evidence from slow-mo cameras and the like, far be it from me to discount it.

I'm sure there is a degree of truth in what both camps say. Perhaps the faster the club is moving, the greater effect the clubhead's path has on the ball's initial direction – or that may be garbage. Anyway, I'm sure it won't be long before mathematicians come up with a scary formula to explain it all.

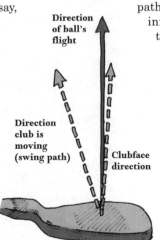

Direction of ball's flight

Direction club is moving (swing path)

Clubface direction

An alternative theory to Jacobs' Ball Flight Laws.

There seems to be a lot of 'most important lessons' in this book. And here's another. Good strategy, or course management, can save you plenty of strokes without you changing a thing in your set-up or swing. You don't even have to practise. All you have to do, in fact, is make better decisions; hit the shots you know you can handle and avoid those you'll never pull off in a million years.

Imagine you're on the tee of a straight, 330-yard par 4 with a narrow fairway bordered on the left by trees and on the right by a lake. The green is small, quick and the pin cut on the right side, just over a deep bunker. You are playing a strokeplay medal round (for matchplay strategy see page 99) so what your opponent or partner gets up to really doesn't matter, nor does the hole's Stroke Index. Which club and what type of shot do you hit?

Weekend golfers will haul the driver out long before they even get to the tee – after all it's a 330-yard hole, so it must be a driver, right? Well, hold on just a minute there tiger; the driver may be the club that gets you

nearest to the green, but you probably can't actually reach it and there's a bit of trouble short of the putting surface in the shape of some shaggy mounds and that deep bunker. Plus, your driver is the

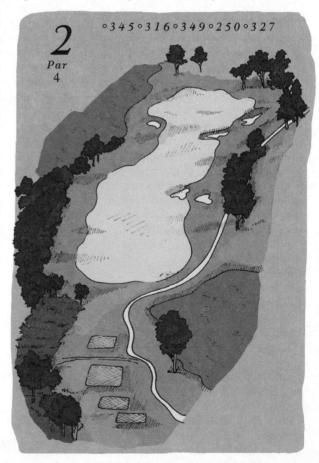

2
Par
4

○345○316○349○250○327

If you have a yardage book that shows the layout of the hole you are about to play, take the time to study it closely (while your opponent's hitting so as not to waste time) and devise a sound strategy for the hole taking your strengths into account and the places you really must avoid.

club that can curve the ball the most, so with the trees and water lurking on either side of the fairway, it could land you in a spot of bother. So why risk it?

Okay, so the driver's back in the bag. How about a 3-wood? Hmm, most amateurs hit their 3-wood every bit as waywardly as the driver so, again, probably not a great choice. In that case, how about a hybrid? Now you're talking. Say you hit a 17° hybrid 200 yards off a tee peg. That will leave you about 120–5 yards to the hole, assuming this course measures its holes to the centre of the green. That's a nice, full 9-iron – a shot you've hit a thousand times before.

So, a hybrid it is then, but what's your line? Well, the pin is tucked behind the bunker on the right so that would suggest going left off the tee to leave yourself a clear line for your approach... but hang on, there are trees over on that side. Good point, we'll veer back towards the centre of the fairway because having to hit a 9-iron over a bunker isn't as bad stymieing yourself behind a sturdy silver birch. So you play a 17° hybrid to the centre of the fairway, a 9-iron slightly behind the hole and two-putt for a par.

If you normally hit a driver and take six you'll have saved yourself two shots with just a moment's deliberation back on the tee. Sensible course management like this really can be the only difference between 105 and 97, 94 and 86, or a sleeve of golf balls and the keys to a new sportscar (or, more realistically, a new driver).

START AT THE HOLE AND WORK BACKWARDS

Always ask yourself: 'which part of the green gives me the easiest putt?' Followed by: 'from which part of the fairway is it easiest to find that part of the green?' And then lastly: 'which club do I need to hit off the tee to put me in that spot in the fairway from which I can find the desired part of the green?' 'Oh,' you may ask, 'can't I just slash away with my driver and be done with it?' If you like, but don't come running to me when you make a double bogey.

Other Considerations

If you're playing a par 5 with bunkers and water up by the green, which you can't possibly reach in two, think seriously about where you want to leave your second shot. If you're more comfortable hitting a 110-yard pitching wedge than a 25-yard lob over water and sand, doesn't it make sense to hit your second to a spot 110 yards short of the green rather than get as close to it as possible?

Always aim to leave yourself an uphill putt, especially if you know the greens are fast. Downhill putts, particularly quick ones, can be very tricky.

If you're in a deep bunker, ask yourself if you've ever got out of one that deep before. If not, swallow your pride and come out sideways. Your attempts to quite literally dig yourself out of trouble might amuse your partners, but you won't be laughing.

It's probably not a good idea to attempt a 240-yard carry over a deep gorge if the furthest you've ever carried a ball is 220 yards.

AT A STRETCH

The swing gurus can harp on about swing planes, swing speed, and swing paths until the cows come home, but if you're not flexible enough to turn, resist, pivot and flex then you're going to have a hard time making a balanced and powerful swing.

I'm no physiotherapist but I do know that as we age our bodies inevitably weaken, become more prone to injuries and get increasingly less flexible.

Golfers on the US Champions Tour still hit it 280 yards off the tee and shoot very impressive scores partly because of improved equipment and partly because the prize money is so great there's plenty of incentive to keep on keeping on. The biggest factor, however, is undoubtedly the high level of fitness and agility these over-50s maintain thanks to regular aerobic workouts and dedicated stretching.

Sadly, putting a club behind our backs, holding each end and twisting a couple of times, or swinging two clubs together on the 1st tee for 30 seconds, just isn't going to be enough. So, to remain flexible and able to swing hard at the ball without pain into your 40s, 50s and beyond, I suggest you commit to a programme of stretching exercises and perform them at least three or four times a week, but preferably every day.

I'm not laying down the law here, just gently nudging you towards the exercise mat or a comfy bit of carpet and encouraging you to do something that, in time, can actually become quite addictive and which will indubitably have a positive effect on your well-being and, far more importantly, your golf.

My Routine

Having recognized the need for daily stretches – I'm not getting any younger, and I've experienced bouts of pretty severe back pain for going on three years now, and my golf swing was actually beginning to hurt – I visited a physiotherapist and borrowed some DVDs from the local library. Going on what the physio told me and what I learned from the DVDs, I put together my own 20-minute routine which I try to complete every day, ideally in the mornings.

If all that sounds a bit keen, bear in mind that it is only 20 minutes. I don't follow it to the letter, and I certainly don't get kitted out in some lime green get-fit outfit, or for that matter the latest hi-tech athletic clothing, I just slip into some shorts and an old T-shirt. But there's no question it helps. Don't get me wrong, I still can't do the splits, but I can get the club pretty high above my head, transfer my weight correctly, hit a ball fairly hard and maintain my balance.

As is the case with anything remotely medical you really need to take account of your own abilities, what suits one person will just as likely have another in spasms for a month. However, there are thousands of books, DVDs and websites (just search for 'golf stretches') out there with countless stretches for people of all ages, physiques and flexibility. Perhaps you could visit a physio like I did, and benefit from some advice that is tailored to your needs.

I merely scratch the surface with my little collection, but it does a job so I'm in no hurry to add any more. So, to get

I Hamstring Stretch 1 – Basically, I make an upturned 'V' with my body, placing my palms face down on the floor and keeping the soles of my feet grounded too.

4 Against a Wall – I simply sit with my back flush against a wall, and I mean flush. I then push my bum up against the wall until I can feel my whole spine pushing against it, and remain in this position for a minute.

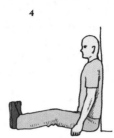

2

Hamstring Stretch 2 – Lying on the floor, I raise one leg to 90° keeping it straight. Pointing my toes at my face, I find a point where I feel some discomfort in my hamstring, and hold this position for 20 seconds before swapping legs.

5 Shoulder Stretch – Placing one arm across my chest, I place my other hand on the elbow of the outstretched arm and pull my arm in towards my chest until I can feel a slight stretch. I hold the position before repeating the stretch on the other arm.

3

Knees to the Side – On my back, I raise my knees, together, off the ground, then move them to one side, and turn my head the other way for an extra 'twist', before stretching the other way.

6 Upper Leg Stretch – Adopting a shoulder-width stance, and holding onto something for support with my left hand, I bring my right foot straight up behind me and grab it with my right hand. I then pull my foot up until I can feel a slight stretch on the front of my thigh. Then I relax, switch and do the other leg.

you thinking along the right lines, here are just a few of my stretches. (Forgive me for not giving them proper names like 'Supine HalfCurl With Lateral Oblique Lunge' – I find all that stuff quite meaningless.)

BAGS, SHOES AND GLOVES

What you carry your clubs in may not be as crucial to your score and enjoyment of the game as the clubs themselves, but it's still important in its own way; as are your choice of footwear and hand-wear. Golf, like most pursuits, is considerably more fun when you're comfortable.

THE CARRY/STAND BAG

Today's young golfers must wonder how those of us getting on in years ever managed to haul our clubs round 18 holes. The bags of my youth were significantly heavier, had a paucity of pockets and no legs so I couldn't just let it fall off my shoulder and have it stand to attention next to my ball.

As a young golfer I had to bend over to put my bag on the ground, and back over again to take out the club of my choice, and back over yet again to pick the bag back up and return it to my shoulder. No wonder I and a good many of my contemporaries now face a life of back pain, medication and physical therapy.

I am staggered every time I read this, but a top of the range carry/stand bag today, such as the Sun Mountain Swift, weighs less than 3lbs! The strap on my 1985 backbreaker probably weighed more than that, and the Swift has got legs! Honestly, 3lbs... with legs!

If that weren't reason enough to roll your eyes and commence a lengthy diatribe about how much tougher life used to be, modern bags have triangular non-slip foot pads 'to resist sinking into the grass and sliding on slick surfaces', two back straps that criss-cross and thereby reduce the pressure on the shoulder on which you habitually carry your bag and even a pen holder. Thank goodness kids today don't have to carry a pencil in their pockets, that's all I can say.

And, of course, bags now come in a veritable palette of colours. In addition to all the usual colours, the Swift is available in russet, cactus and Baltic (red, green and blue to you and me), while Ogio's Vaporlite comes in juice, petrol, garnet, flame and even chiaro – go look it up.

CART BAGS

For golfers who can no longer carry their clubs and play with the help of a motorized trolley or buggy, weight and legs aren't so much of an issue. Sure, the heavier your bag the sooner your motorized trolley's battery is going to pack up, but it's no big deal if your bag weighs a few more pounds than it could. And if you travel by buggy, what the hell, get a 10lb tour bag with room enough for your entire wardrobe and a couple of pets.

This bag can hold your clubs, your raingear, about 30 golf balls, an umbrella, your snacks, your gloves, keys, wallet and sunscreen, and still weigh less than my old bag, empty. And it can probably do your laundry too.

A modern golf shoe is stylish, comfortable and grips the ground like glue.

SHOES

It goes without saying that golf's technological revolution has had a major influence on shoes as well. Kilties, the strange, leather flaps on top of the shoe whose purpose was never made clear to me (it surely can't have been style) have thankfully been consigned to the dim and distant past, though a few manufacturers won't banish them altogether and still offer kiltied pairs, mostly in their women's ranges.

Thanks to vastly improved chassis design, better sole grips (rubber cleats now that metal spikes have also been cast out) and foam or gel-moulded uppers, the stability, balance and comfort of a golf shoe can't be compared with yesterday's stiff, poorly balanced shoes. Actually, they can: today's shoes are great; those from a generation ago were rubbish.

Modern shoes can get pretty dear though, especially if you're looking at Footjoy Classics and other top-of-the-range shoes; however, there are plenty of good-value shoes to be had. I get by with a pair of old GreenJoys, but if I were in the market for a new pair I'd probably opt for the Adidas Tour 360.

GLOVES

Two years ago, I purchased a glove boasting anatomical relief pads said to increase comfort and decrease friction, a pre-rotated finger design to promote the natural motion of my fingers and strategic index-to-hand motion and web interface zones to... well, who knows what they were for?

Shortly after buying this, I discovered it was illegal for use in competition largely because it was simply too advanced and put users of other, less futuristic gloves at a serious disadvantage. At least, that's how I read the ruling.

I can't help thinking the game's rules makers (the United States Golf Association in the US and the Royal and Ancient Golf Club everywhere else) were a little premature in this instance because I'm as wayward and inconsistent as I ever was prior to purchasing it. Somehow I'm just not reaping the benefits of those strategic web interface zones.

My advice is not to waste too much time worrying about your choice of glove. To put it simply, leather gloves might cost a bit more than synthetic micro-fibre all-weather gloves, but won't be turning anyone into Tiger Woods.

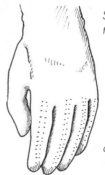

Some players prefer not to wear a glove but I think that's because they grew up playing without one and just got used to it. If they ever tried one on, they'd probably discover a whole new world of grip and control.

WARMING UP RIGHT

The practice ground is perhaps my favourite place to go when attending a professional tournament. Here you'll see all the top players in fairly relaxed mode hitting far more shots than you'll ever see them hit out on the course.

But the range is worth finding for another reason. Observe closely and you'll learn a very important lesson; the warm-up isn't a time for reckless swings with the driver, but a structured session that hardly ever changes from day to day.

While the typical golfer's warm-up may involve nothing more arduous than a sprint from the car to the 1st tee and a few superficial stretches that really just make him feel a bit dizzy, the pros' systematic approach to warming up sees them arrive at the range an hour or so before their tee-time.

After several minutes' of proper, effective stretching, a pro will invariably pull out the sand wedge and hit a few pitches. It's a slow start that allows the muscles to get used to the idea they are wanted for another round of golf. Having loosened up a bit, the pro will begin working through the clubs, eventually reaching the driver, but probably only hitting four or five shots.

Many pros hit the same number of balls with each club – three fades, three draws, three high, three low and three regular shots with a pitching wedge, then an 8-iron, then a 6 and so on. It's also common to see them work their way back up through the bag after hitting the driver, finishing with a short iron so they can establish a rhythm for the day.

The pro will head to the short-game area maybe half an hour before tee-time and hit a number of chips, pitches, lobs and bunker shots. At Tee minus 15 minutes, the pro will stop at the practice putting green. Just as it was on the range, the task here is not to practise, but rather build a smooth tempo and also get a feel for the speed of the surfaces. Then a finish with a few short, easy putts, will help give

The pro's warm-up is relaxed, not hurried; hitting balls for 30 minutes or so establishing a rhythm for the day, and ending up on the practice putting green.

a very strong mental picture of the ball dropping into the hole.

The root cause of many amateurs' weaknesses out on the course can be found in their warm-ups. So here is a direct comparison between the structured routine a pro will run through, and the haphazard five minutes that many amateurs make do with. Which do you recognize?

PRO'S WARM-UP
+ Arrives an hour before tee-time
+ Several effective stretches
+ Starts with sand wedge
+ Hits 30–40 shots in total
+ Spends 15 mins on short-game
+ Hits a couple of chip shots on the 1st tee perhaps
+ Spends 15 mins putting
+ Starts feeling relaxed and loose

AMATEUR'S WARM-UP
+ Arrives five mins before tee-time
+ Touches toes a couple of times
+ Starts with driver
+ Hits as many shots as will fit into two mins
+ Hits a couple of chips and a couple of putts on the 1st tee perhaps
+ Starts feeling stressed and stiff

TEN-MINUTE WARM-UP
If other activities prevent you from arriving an hour before you start, at least do a few decent stretches (see pages 32–3), hit a few chips and putts on or around the putting green and make a few smooth swings with the club you will be hitting off the 1st tee, trying to clip a few blades of grass and focusing on tempo and balance.

Go Easy on Your Greenkeeper

We watch the Masters on TV and want greens just like Augusta's. We see European Tour players taking on 7,500-yard courses and want the course we play on lengthened. We watch the Players Championship from the TPC of Sawgrass with its exciting, if a little gimmicky, island green and wonder when we're going to get ours.

Moves to recreate these conditions are often reckless and ill-conceived, however. What we tend to forget is that Augusta National (home of the Masters) has an almost limitless budget, a greenkeeping staff of dozens, it closes for half the year, it probably hosts a fifth the number of rounds that most courses do (or a tenth in the case of municipals) and the weather in Georgia is normally pretty good. Everything that your course isn't, hasn't or doesn't in fact.

Extending courses is counter-productive because 99 per cent of golfers have no business playing any course over 7,000 yards. They couldn't reach many of the par 4s let alone par 5s and rounds would become that bit longer at a time when people's recreational time is getting shorter. Plus building new tees is really expensive which, as we've seen before, means higher green fees and higher membership subscriptions.

As for Sawgrass and its island green; do you really want to lose half a dozen balls at a single hole?

⛳ PICKING A PRO

Tiger Woods has one. Jack Nicklaus had one in the prime of his career. Nick Faldo went from under-achieving journeyman to multi-major winner after finding the right man for him. Tom Watson, Arnold Palmer, Bobby Jones, Seve Ballesteros, Greg Norman and Annika Sorenstam all have had or still have one. Could it be that you need a teacher too?

While it's true certain players don't benefit from formal coaching, I am almost willing to bet my house you would become a more competent golfer by taking lessons, especially if you haven't been playing long.

Beginners need to learn the fundamentals before proceeding to the full swing, while seasoned players require if not constant observation then at least occasional confirmation that their set-up is sound. Nicklaus used to start each season with a lesson from his man Jack Grout just to make sure his basics had survived the winter. And if it's good enough for the Golden Bear, it is most assuredly good enough for the rest of us.

So Who You Gonna Call?

It's probably okay for total beginners to phone the nearest course, range, golf centre or academy (incidentally, when did places where you learn golf start calling themselves 'Academies', and the guys that run these places 'Deans'? I mean, it's not ballet or military exercises we're learning here) and ask for the least expensive pro to take them out and show them the ropes. It's likely you'll get a 17-year-old apprentice, but he should be able to get you holding the club and standing to the ball correctly at least.

If you build a good rapport with Junior and are confident he can take you to the next stage by all means stick with him. I've seen enough nightmare situations though – I was responsible for plenty myself during my time as an overly eager young teacher – to suggest you find someone with a little more experience to take over from here. What you definitely, absolutely, positively do not want is a young chap who thinks he knows it all (something I've definitely been guilty of in the past) teaching you to swing like Tiger Woods. If you had Woods's physical attributes then perhaps you could swing like him; but you don't, so you can't.

Group classes are a good option for beginners. You learn the basics but pay a fraction of the cost of individual lessons.

Experience

Find a pro who has seen it all before – every swing and every body type – and who can take what ability you have and maximize your potential.

The Lesson from Hell

I recount the following story knowing full well that ten years previously the young teacher could have been me and the pupil any one of the poor, defenceless souls that came to me for lessons.

One bright, sunny day a few summers ago I was at the driving range when I became aware of a lesson going on in the bay next to mine. A very young assistant pro was instructing a middle-aged woman whom I suspect hadn't been playing for more than a month.

I couldn't help listening in and was astonished to hear the pro talk about swing planes, resistance and leverage. The woman clearly felt some discomfort every time she tried to keep her right knee bent while reaching for the roof with her hands. She grimaced when trying to maintain her body angles throughout the swing.

According to the textbook, the pro was right all along. But according to the feedback he should have picked up from his charge's expressions, my guess is this lesson did nothing to encourage her back.

Unless you're playing off scratch, a good teacher won't ask you to pronate your forearms or resist the turn of the upper body against relatively static hips. A good teacher will keep it simple and appropriate for your level. A good teacher will notice your belly sticking over your trouser belt or your troublesome back, and will have asked about your six-day-a-week job and how little time you have to practise. A good teacher will ask what it is you hope to achieve from your lessons, and will be able to tell you whether your aspirations are realistic. And rather than take you on the two-year swing-building odyssey that Faldo embarked upon with David Leadbetter, your wise old hand will offer suggestions as to how you can make your faulty, but impossibly deep-rooted, swing still work for you.

BOTTOM LINE

One point worth remembering is that your pro has every right to expect some effort on your part. No matter how good any pro is, if you aren't going to practise what you're told, you may as well not bother showing up.

Ask questions, be clear about what is being suggested and practise whatever you learn. But if it's obvious your pro is asking something of your body that it clearly isn't capable of, I suggest you look elsewhere.

A veteran pro can work with what little you've got and still make you a strong player.

There's a well-known story about a kid who, watching golf for the first time, asks his father watching with him why the players always try to miss their first putt and then knock the second putt in. And I suppose until you learn just how testing putting can be, the question is a fair one.

On the face of it, tapping a small ball towards a hole three times as wide, across a carefully maintained surface with a tool devised by one of the world's top metallurgists really shouldn't be as difficult as we make it. And it certainly shouldn't cause uncontrollable psychological and muscular twitches – the yips (see page 98) – in otherwise normal, healthy human beings.

I believe thinking that putting is easy actually helps make it so. A reliance on expensive putters and convoluted training aids just seems to make it more complicated than it need be.

No two putters (the people, not the clubs) are alike. If you watched Bernhard Langer circa 1990, Chris DiMarco and Phil Mickelson putting, and didn't know any better, you might not think they were all trying to achieve the same thing. Some crouch, some stand tall. Some use a conventional reverse overlap grip, while an increasing number don't. And some allow the putterhead to move back and through on a smaller version of their full swing arc, while others move it straight back and through. But as with the full swing, good results start with a set of fixed fundamentals that you really must adhere to if you want to get the ball in the hole sooner rather than later.

GRIP AND SET-UP

✦ First, get comfortable and spread your weight evenly between both feet.

✦ Grip the putter how you like (see below) but generally your palms should face each other. Grip the club lightly. With the standard reverse overlap method, the putter grip should rest in the palm of your left hand and the shaft point straight up your left arm so it appears to be an extension of the forearm.

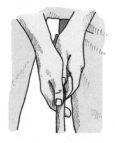

Reverse Overlap. Index finger of left hand rests on middle fingers of right hand. Both thumbs on top.

Cross-handed. Left hand below right, again thumbs on top.

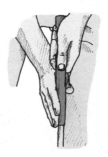

The Claw.

The Claw Mk II.

- I've seen good putters whose feet were open or closed to the target line, but everyone's shoulders are square.
- Some good putters have their eyes inside the target line, but no good putter ever positioned them outside the line. Most position their eye directly over the ball, or try to.
- Position the ball forward of centre, how much is up to you. I've seen some put it opposite their left big toe, but I don't know of any good putters who position the ball behind centre.

THE STROKE

Only your shoulders, arms and hands should move; while your knees, waist and head remain totally still. (Envisage the 'Y' formed by the putter and your arms remaining fixed throughout.) The backswing and follow-through should be roughly the same length – accelerate the putterhead through the ball.

The speed and tempo of the stroke should remain constant for all putts. All that changes is the length of stroke: the longer the putt, the further the putterhead moves back and through.

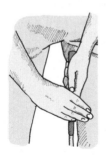

The Claw Mk III.

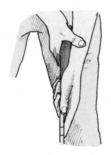

Bernhard Langer resorted to this after numerous bouts of the yips. Hey, whatever works, right?

⚑ HIT DOWN TO HIT UP

This concept is touched upon in 'Ball Position', again in 'Backspin' and a number of other places, but it is still worthy of its own entry. It is, after all, so very, very important.

At first it may sound strange, and indeed in many other sports, if you want the ball to go up, you hit the ball, well... up. In this game the clubhead of a short or medium

Ball first, ground second.

iron (the driver should be rising as it contacts the ball sitting on a tee, and long irons should ideally sweep the ball off the ground without taking much of a divot) should be moving downward when it strikes the ball. This creates the backspin that helps the ball climb steeply into the air and stop quickly on the green.

By positioning the ball correctly, somewhere between the centre of your stance and opposite your left heel (see page 22) and then transferring your weight properly on to the instep of your back foot in the backswing and forward on to the front foot in the downswing (nearly all your weight should be on your front foot with your waist facing the target at the end of your swing), you should strike the ball moments before the club reaches the low point on its swing arc.

You won't believe me, but at the start of the 20th century, golfers were extremely well dressed. They still looked pretty spiffy well into the 1930s and 40s. So when did it all go wrong?

First, a little history. A hundred years ago, the golfer's wardrobe consisted of collared shirts, ties and tweedy jackets. When standards began dropping (that may be harsh, let's say dipping) in the 1920s, golfers soon realized they could hit the ball further simply by removing their starchy outer garments, and that wearing something with a bit of colour wasn't illegal. Slowly, the white, long-sleeved shirt was replaced by short-sleeved, soft-collared T-shirts and jackets by either cardigans or sweaters.

Smart, formal, dapper even. Shame he couldn't get his hands above his head without ripping a sleeve.

EXPRESS YOURSELF

Sartorially, golfers began parting ways in the 1940s and 50s. Virtually identical up to that point, many players remained elegant while others began to express their inner dazzle. So while Sam Snead and Ben Hogan preferred understated class, Jimmy Demaret would take trips to New York to shop for vividly coloured shirts and slacks.

Next, while Arnold Palmer, Jack Nicklaus and Gary Player were keeping it simple (although Player did once slip on a pair of trousers with one black leg and one white leg), Demaret's garishly saddled shoes were being filled by Doug Sanders, the Peacock, who missed a tiny putt on the 18th green at St Andrews in the 1970 Open Championship that would have won him the title. He lost the next day in a play-off with Nicklaus and, with all due respect, I'm glad he did. I mean, can you imagine someone wearing tight, plum-coloured trousers and a bright pinky-orange cardigan holding aloft the Claret Jug? The very idea...

IT ONLY GETS WORSE

Of course, the less said about the rest of the '70s the better, although it's worth pointing out the style-free fashions of the decade sealed golf's reputation for poor dress sense seemingly forever.

The '80s and '90s saw only minor improvements. Yes, the orange-and-green checked, flared trousers Tom Watson wore when winning the 1977 Open (held up by a ghastly white belt, which has somehow made an unwelcome return to the game) had been replaced by more restrained khakis. But these were shapeless and, worse, pleated. Shirts became horribly baggy with sleeves coming down a few inches lower than the elbow. Not only could you play golf in them, you could camp out in them too.

THE LINDBERG EXPLOSION

At the start of this century, Sweden's Jesper Parnevik spurned the baggy look in favour of tighter, shorter-sleeved, shirts and flat-front trousers designed by

On the right golfer, short-sleeved, figure-hugging shirts work well.

Stockholm's J. Lindberg. Parnevik had the frame suited to closer-fitting clothes and for the first time in 30 years a professional golfer looked cool. But now every Tom, Dick, Justin, Sergio and Mikko is out there with the drain-pipe orange trousers, obligatory white belt and tight shirts. And while it shows some progress, seeing the occasional fat bloke in figure-hugging attire is less than appetizing.

But it's not just the big-boned who should stay clear. Old, bad and infrequent golfers should reject it too. The Lindberg Look is strictly for the young, slim professional – the rest of us just look silly.

KEEP IT SIMPLE

My policy, for as long as I can remember, has been to mimic what I wear to work on the golf course. That means bland khakis (and the occasional slightly more elaborate pair of slacks), unfussy shirts and black or brown shoes. If you really want to wear more decorative clothing, like England's Ian Poulter for instance, then you had better have the game to back it

up. I'd say you need to be playing off five or better to justify the attention a Lindberg print will get you, and get down to scratch before wrapping a white belt around a pair of neon trousers won't outshine your game.

Mock Turtles

Not an indie-rock band from Manchester, Lewis Carroll's fictional character, or even a Victorian soup. Golf's version of the mock turtle is, in fact, a sweater that resembles a polo-neck and which Tiger Woods made popular a few years back. Comfortable, stylish, warm and not too dressy, it works as well on the high street as it does the golf course. It still doesn't quite suit the guy whose belly droops over his belt, though. But then, what does?

The mock turtle looks good especially on a certain Tiger Woods.

ON THE SLOPES

A lot of instruction books put shots from sloping lies in the 'Trouble Shots' chapter; but they really needn't be any trouble at all.

These shots are all about balance. Make a few minor adjustments to your address position, and a short, compact swing and you'll do fine.

WHEN YOU'RE HITTING UPHILL:

+ Take more club. Hitting uphill means a longer shot, effectively. The steeper the slope the more club you need.
+ Tilt your right shoulder down a little and flex your right knee slightly more than usual. This prevents too steep an attack on the ball.
+ Play the ball in the middle of your stance and aim a little right as the tendency is to pull the shot.
+ Don't let your weight hang back on your back foot. Push it forward on to the front foot as normal.

WHEN YOU'RE HITTING DOWNHILL:

+ Take less club as shooting downhill effectively shortens the shot.
+ Tilt your left shoulder down a little and straighten your right leg a touch.
+ Play the ball an inch back of centre, and aim slightly left of your target as the ball has a tendency to fade.

+ Again, let your weight move on to your front foot and feel like the club moves down the slope after impact.

WHEN THE BALL IS ABOVE YOUR FEET:

+ Aim right as the slope will encourage a pull or hooked shot.
+ The ball is closer to you so grip well down the handle.
+ Play the ball in the centre or an inch back of centre.
+ Push your weight forward slightly as it will want to fall back down the slope on to your heels.

WHEN THE BALL IS BELOW YOUR FEET:

+ Aim left of your target as this shot will want to move left to right in the air.
+ Put a little more flex in your knees and tilt a little more from the hips.
+ Grip the club at the top of the handle.
+ Again, play the ball in the centre or slightly to the right of centre.
+ Place a bit more weight on your heels.

Sloping lies call for a few alterations to your usual set-up and a shorter swing to help you keep your balance.

HEROES

Golf is so hard to master, amateurs can't help but look on wide-eyed when they see the world's best crack a driver down the fairway.

I'm at an age now where I don't really have heroes, at least not in the sense that I want to be Tiger Woods when I grow up. I no longer idolize but respect such players. I could happily watch Woods on the practice ground all day, and who wouldn't admire the work he does for his charitable foundation and learning centre? But I don't have a huge Tiger poster on my bedroom wall, a Tiger headcover or a Tiger screensaver.

That said, I must admit to keeping a Seve Ballesteros scrapbook when I was younger. It couldn't have lasted more than a couple of months and was randomly cobbled together – just a few photos and clippings – but it kept me busy for a while and helped strengthen my love for the game. Today, Woods is similarly revered by kids around the world, and it's only to be hoped that such a great role model should help cement the next generation's love for the game.

I wouldn't mind it a bit if my kid chose Tiger Woods for a hero.

Uniqueness

Far too many golf courses are guilty of marketing misinformation and near hysterical hype when promoting their layouts. I mean, just how many 'unique' golf courses can there be? And exactly which championships has your 'Championship Course' hosted lately?

This 'problem' is out of control in the US and getting worse in the UK. I recently read of a new course in England that not only claimed to be unique but also entirely natural despite having been 'created' by one of the world's top course architects. How do you create something entirely natural?

I understand these courses are trying to attract business, and that's not a crime; but the truth of the matter is that too many of these 'unique' courses have very little to distinguish them from dozens of others.

No golf course is unique, not even the Old Course at St Andrews. It's a links course, a very special links course, but still one of over 200 of its type in the world. The closest I've seen to unique was a nine-hole course somewhere in South Australia whose name I forget. It was laid out over a wide expanse of dirt, its greens small squares of bitumen that softened in the midday sun, and into which I sunk. If this is unique, then I'm not sure that uniqueness is something worth shouting about.

PLAY A LINKS

Britain and Ireland are fortunate to have a virtual monopoly on links courses. If you've never experienced their very particular charms and challenges then I urge you to stop whatever you're doing (reading this book presumably), get on the phone and make a tee-time at a links course, any one will do.

It might look bleak and fairly uninviting to begin with, but if you haven't played a links before you'll understand what all the fuss is about by the time you reach the 3rd tee.

WHAT IS A LINKS?

Some say a river estuary, or firth, must be close or that there should be nine holes out to a distant point and nine back to the clubhouse. Others maintain it must be hard by the sea with views of the water from most, if not all, the holes.

There are just too many exceptions to these rules for me though. The bottom line really is coastal sand dunes on which fine fescue grasses grow, but which sustain very few trees. Low-lying bushes, principally gorse, are common, however, and the ground is usually undulating, the turf firm and fast thanks to its exceptional drainage and the bunkers deep enough to prevent the fine sand being blown away. And, because most of them are very old, links courses are almost entirely natural with none of the artificial frills such as ponds, lakes, fountains, waterfalls and flowerbeds so common on modern courses. Also,

you can expect a handful of blind shots where the drive or approach shot has to clear a dune.

Are links courses bleak? Certainly, on a grey winter's day, they can be downright desolate. Are they unfair? Sure they are, you can hit a perfect drive only to watch it rebound off a small mound into the rough. Are they quirky? Absolutely, some links holes are just plain weird. But these are all the reasons why we love them so much.

WHAT A LINKS DEFINITELY IS NOT

Because of the global appeal of the Open Championship and the popularity of golf trips to Britain and Ireland, links courses are practically revered around the world. So it's no great surprise marketers who don't really have a clue what a links course is apply the term to virtually any course with a few mounds, a bit of wind and a lack of trees.

It doesn't matter how many fake mounds a course has though, how much wind blows through it or how few trees there are; if it's not on or near the coast, doesn't play over undulating sand dunes and its turf is soft and lush, then it doesn't make the list.

HOW TO PLAY LINKS GOLF

I'm really not the man to be telling you how to play a links as I've had precious little success on them. The best I've ever shot over the dunes, in fact, was 75 at Southport and Ainsdale many, many moons ago. If, like me, you're used to playing an inland parkland course with its broad-leafed grass, tree-lined fairways and artificial water hazards, then playing a links course is the equivalent of moving from Roland Garros to Wimbledon. It's a totally different form of the game that requires a whole new approach.

You need to take advantage if you're teeing off downwind, and you need to know how not to fight the wind when it's in your face. A few adjustments might well be necessary when putting too (see page 100).

Fairway lies tend to be very tight and firm, and if you make contact with the ball slightly before hitting the turf and take a shallow divot you should create sufficient backspin to hold the equally firm greens. With irons, you should play the ball in the middle of your stance – hands ahead, shaft angled forward – and feel like you squeeze the ball off the turf.

Off such tight lies, and also in the bunkers, you will need a sand wedge with very little bounce. Indeed, it might be better to use your lob wedge out of the sand. Play the ball a little further back in your stance than normal and come down quite steeply and slightly closer to the ball than you would at an inland course where the sand is typically light and fluffy. It is much finer and denser at a links so if you enter too far behind the ball the club will probably skim across the surface and you'll blade the shot straight into the 6ft revetted wall in front of you.

Finally, if your ball bounces at a funny, unexpected angle off a bump in the fairway and rolls into a bunker, don't say that every book and magazine article you've ever read about links courses didn't warn you.

If you're unlucky enough to encounter a bunker face like this I would highly recommend coming out backwards.

HOLE·IN·ONE

Don't think for a second I'm going to give you any tips on how to make a hole-in-one, except perhaps to 'hit it straight at the hole with the right club'. You see, despite hitting the pin, the rim and the flag itself on any number of occasions, an 'ace' has eluded me all these years.

Walter, a native of Japan but now living in Honolulu, was in no hurry to celebrate his hole-in-one. Despite it being the first of his life and coming at an age when he was unlikely to make another, he quietly picked his ball out of the hole, put it in his pocket and started off for the next tee.

'For Heaven's sake Walter,' I lamented. 'You just made a hole-in-one. Aren't you going to at least tip your cap to an imaginary gallery?'

Walter looked at me sternly and, because of the language barrier, lifted his finger to his lips and uttered something that needed no English on his part or Japanese on mine for me to understand: 'Shhhh,' he said, shaking his head.

As Walter strode off, his friend Toshio, the eldest of the three retired Japanese bankers with whom I had been grouped, walked over and explained. 'When you're playing in England, are you meant to buy everyone in the clubhouse a drink after a hole-in-one?'

'Absolutely,' I said.

'Well, this is the busiest course in the world; and there are a lot of people in the clubhouse.'

I could see the course was packed, but I hadn't the faintest idea that Ala Wai GC – a couple of miles from Waikiki Beach – was the busiest course in the world. Now that I did, I knew where Walter was coming from.

But on reflection, I doubt very much that I could have been so reticent and maintained my composure quite like Walter. I suspect, in fact, I might have done something really silly like climb a tree, dive into a pond or do some ridiculous Chi Chi Rodriguez-style dance with the flagstick.

As Good as it Gets

I've come close to making an ace several times, but the blessed ball has never dropped. A few days after the round with my new retired Japanese banker buddies I was at a course with one of those only-in-Hawaii-type par 3s: mountains covered in lush jungle to my right, turquoise ocean to my left and a 200-yard-wide inlet between the tee and green in which waves crashed against the rocks. To say it was postcard material doesn't do it justice, and a hole-in-one at this hole, of all holes, would surely rank very high on one's list of memorable lifetime achievements.

My ball came within two inches of giving me dinner conversation material for years to come. Okay, it would have become dull at some point, but like any golfer, I could have embellished the story to include a couple of whales breaching in the bay below, and perhaps a brutal tempest moving in off the ocean.

My ball came so close to going in that a guy standing on his villa balcony 50 yards to the right of the green threw his hands in the air and screamed 'Yeeeeeeooooowwwwwhhhhh' as it rolled towards the hole, caught the lip and spun out.

You know, I pay my taxes, I repair two pitch marks on most greens that I come to, and I even feed the ducks occasionally on cold winter days. I deserve a hole-in-one. And when I read about a Californian woman who claims to have made 16 in 2007 alone I can't help but feel just a little snubbed.

After an ace on a hole like this, I might retire my clubs to the attic forever. Apart from winning a major, could the game get much sweeter?

WATCH TIGER WOODS

He's still got a little way to go to reach Jack Nicklaus' record of 18 pro major championships but, assuming he remains healthy, it's only a matter of time before he does. Surely he's the finest player ever, and until you see him play you have no idea how hard and how purely a golf ball can be struck.

At the 2000 Open Championship, played on the Old Course at St Andrews, I had the good fortune to follow Woods for all 18 holes of his second round, inside the ropes – a privilege afforded members of the press. His 66 looked utterly routine. He never missed a shot and by the end of play he led by three. By the time he was handed the Claret Jug on Sunday evening, he was eight shots ahead of second place.

Watching Woods play is a seminal moment in a golf fan's life. To a non-golfer that will sound absurd, but I think it's a shame they can't appreciate just how brilliant Woods is. You can always remember the time(s) you saw him play and most of the shots he hit. I suppose it must have been the same watching Sobers or DiMaggio swing a bat, Pele kick a football, Ali land a punch, Schumacher round a bend, Hinault or Armstrong climb L'Alpe D'Huez, Spitz win Gold, Red Rum negotiate Beecher's Brook or Sampras fire a cross-court forehand.

The crack of impact when Woods hits a driver is unlike any sound you will have heard on a golf course before. Unless the sky is blue and the sun behind you, it's unlikely you'll be able to follow the flight of his ball, for a few holes at least while your eyes adjust. You mouth crude words when you see how high and how far he hits his irons and you shake your head at his delicate touch around the greens. His putting? Let's just say don't ever bet on him missing, no matter how far away he is.

I would suggest a few things to look out for that might help you with your own game. But apart from his textbook address position and how still he keeps his head when putting, I'm not sure any connection can be made between his game and ours. Just take whatever opportunity you get to watch him and go home satisfied you saw the best golfer that ever lived.

Tiger Woods in full flight is an awesome sight.

MAKING LISTS

Pick up a copy of any major golf publication and you can't help but notice that the world of golf is rankings mad.

The charm of St Enodoc in Rock, Cornwall, England is almost too much to bear.

The cynic in me says a large part of the reason these rankings exist is to stimulate advertising revenue, and give each issue a snappy cover line; and while there's more than a grain of truth in that they also provoke a lot of feisty debate in the clubhouse bar – my top three, by the way, are the Brancaster, the Bunker Bar at Bandon Dunes and the modest but perfectly appointed bar in the men's locker room at Bay Hill in Florida, where I once spent an afternoon sipping cocktails and playing cards with my partners from the morning. For what it's worth, here are my ten favourite courses:

+ St Enodoc, England
+ West Lancashire, England
+ Narin and Portnoo, Ireland
+ Kingston Heath, Australia
+ Black Mesa, USA
+ North Berwick, Scotland
+ Old Course, St Andrews, Scotland
+ Royal Portrush, Ireland
+ Bandon Dunes, USA
+ Walton Heath (Old), England

DAWN OR DUSK?

If, like me, you're at your physical and mental best well after midday, playing golf shortly after dawn is all too rare a treat. But as all golfers know, it's easier to be up at 6am for a tee-time than at 9am to go to work.

If circumstances were different, very different – no family, no job, a body that functioned properly before mid-morning and so on – I'd play all my golf between the hours of 5.00 and 8.30am. This is a magical time when the rising sun hasn't yet grown uncomfortably hot and the early morning light gives the colours of the grass, trees, flowers and sky an intensity you just don't get later in the day. The fresh, cool dew cleans the air, the greenstaff are whirring into action and, without taking up where William Wordsworth left off, the birds are singing, and all is right with the world.

If you've never played golf at this time of day, I suggest you try it at least once this summer. However, if that's really not for you, if you have a hard time waking up, showering, breakfasting and driving to the course before sun-up then don't worry, late summer evenings are almost as good. The course is emptying, the light

equally sublime and by the time you walk in off the 18th green, the bar's open.

Golf at dawn, a real treat.

CELEBRATING THE RIGHT WAY

Hole a 15ft putt on the last green to win the club championship and it's likely you're going to react. But you don't want your win to be remembered only for the ludicrous celebration you unloaded as the putt dropped.

At the 1990 US Open at Medinah in Chicago, 45-year-old Hale Irwin had a monster putt on the 72nd green to take the clubhouse lead. The ball took forever to cross the wickedly fast putting surface but eventually toppled in, whereupon Irwin set off on a mad dash around the gallery whooping, hollering and high-fiving.

After holing a curly birdie putt on the final green, which he himself later admitted never looked like it was going in, Seve Ballesteros won the 1984 Open Championship at St Andrews, and went into his famous 360° conquering matador routine.

Both celebrations were a touch excessive perhaps but, given the context, entirely justified. Irwin hadn't won a major for 11 years and became the oldest winner of the US Open. Seve's second Claret Jug came at his favourite course after beating two of his biggest rivals in Bernhard Langer and Tom Watson. Plus, he always was a bit of a showboat.

> ## Celebratory Don'ts in Club Competitions
>
> + Do not doff your cap – no one's looking.
> + Do not throw your ball to the gallery – no one's there to catch it.
> + Do not throw your hat into the air – save that for graduation day.
> + Do not stand still with both arms raised for more than three seconds.
> + Do not jump up and down, run to the cup (run anywhere for that matter), blow any kisses, look at your partners with a sort of 'Take that!' gesture, point at the hole, dive into any ponds, moonwalk or wave the flag around in the air.
> + On no account start crying.

You may be something of an exhibitionist yourself, but I'm afraid your win just doesn't warrant such excess. In most individual club competitions, anything more than a single fist pump and a whispered 'Yes!' is generally considered vulgar. If you're playing in a team competition, however, and you hole the putt that wins the overall match, by all means pump your fist twice, maybe three times, and embrace your teammates. No, on second thoughts, just shake their hands and, if you must, slap their backs. Whatever you do though, do it after having shaken your opponent's hand.

For heaven's sake calm down.
You're embarrassing yourself.

THE BASIC PITCH

On and around the green is where club golfers can make quick inroads into their handicap. The 50–80-yard pitch shot is a stock short-game shot that club golfers will need five or six times a round, possibly more. So it would be to your very great advantage were you to master it.

LOFTED PITCH

Most of the distance between the ball and the hole is covered in the air. If contact is pure, you're playing from a nice firm lie and hitting a high-spinning ball, it should bounce one or twice before stopping abruptly.

✦ Use your sand wedge or lob wedge (60°) and play the ball roughly midway between your feet or perhaps an inch or two back of that. Your hands should be ahead of the ball with the shaft angled forward slightly.

Play the ball in the centre of your stance, hands forward, to promote the necessary downward strike. Swing back allowing your wrists to break a little and keep your head still. Finish facing the target.

✦ Grip down the club a little and stand closer to the ball than normal with your feet closer together. Open your stance slightly and press a little more weight onto the front foot.

✦ With soft, supple arms – definitely not stiff and rigid – and allowing your wrists to hinge naturally, hit down making contact with the ball first then the ground. There should be a small but pronounced shift of weight, so finish on your front foot with your waist facing the target.

✦ To gauge how long your swing should be and how hard you need to hit the ball in order for it to travel the desired distance, I'm afraid you will have to practise.

RUNNING PITCH

To hit a slightly lower, flatter shot that runs more along the ground (useful if the hole is cut at the back of the green and you're near the front), use a pitching wedge or 9-iron. Bear in mind if you have a bad lie and can't generate much backspin, the running shot with a less-lofted club is the better option. If the pin is at the front but you have a bad lie and can't play the more lofted pitch, accept the fact that 20–30ft past the hole may be the best you can do.

READING THE GREENS

I could give you a few pointers on what to look for when reading greens, but when it comes to actually judging how hard to hit the putt and on what line it should start, I'm afraid you're on your own.

The best green-readers have a sixth sense that allows them to visualize how much a putt will break when hit at a certain speed. It's partly innate, but you can certainly become a better judge of speed, and therefore line, with experience and practice. But even with this skill, you still need to consider the effect certain conditions will have on your putt. I reckon most people instinctively pick up on the following factors, but it doesn't hurt to say them again:

Begin analyzing your putt as you approach the green. There is a lot you can learn from a distance.

+ The shorter the grass, the quicker the putt, of course.
+ Early morning dew, or indeed any moisture, will slow a putt.
+ The darker the shade of green, the slower the putt.
+ The coarser the grass, the slower the putt.
+ Greens will probably be slightly slower late in the day than they were in the morning.

It pays to start reading the green as you approach it. I've heard it said the best place to get a good indication of a green's contours is from 20 yards away. Note any significant slopes, the colour of the grass, firmness of the ground and wind (yes, wind affects putts). Feed all this into your on-board computer, hit return and you should be left with a very clear picture of your ball rolling into the hole.

There is another more scientific way to read the line of your putt than by simply bending down and looking at it.

A handful of pros do it today, and several greats from the past did it. However, Tiger doesn't and nor do I; not because Tiger doesn't you understand, but because I don't really know how to.

PLUMB-BOBBING
To plumb-bob correctly, you need to discover which is your dominant eye. The simplest way is to form a circle with your thumb and index finger and stretch out your arm. Position the circle so there is a distant object in the centre. Then close each eye in turn and whichever eye you can still see the object with, or the one that moves it the least, is your dominant eye.

Now stand a few feet behind your ball, on a direct line with the hole. Hold your putter up at arm's length and let it hang vertically. Look with your dominant eye and hold the putter so the shaft cuts through the ball. Whichever side of the shaft the ball appears on is the direction in which the putt will break. Whether this actually shows you something new, or simply confirms a line that you had already assessed intuitively depends on who you listen to. Plenty of people believe in it; but, like I say, I don't do it.

PLAY MORE BREAK

Amateurs tend to miss breaking putts on the low side of the hole. We're often told to aim at the apex of a putt – the point at which the curve is greatest. But if we aim at that point the ball will most likely already be below it by the time it draws level. Because they travel faster immediately after impact, putts move fairly straight early on and curve back to the hole as they lose momentum. But a putt will break some before it reaches what we think is the apex. And that means if you aim at the apex your putt starts on the wrong line. It's difficult to say exactly how much more break amateurs should play, but rest assured you need to play more break.

If you know what you're doing and don't waste any time you should at least try plumb-bobbing. It could confirm your initial thoughts on which way the putt might break.

A Word About Grain

Ten years ago in Harare, before Mugabe wrecked the place, I played on greens with so much grain (the tendency of grass to grow in a certain direction) that reading putts was next to impossible. I would see a considerable right-to-left break but my playing partner, a local, would insist the putt broke left to right. Never quite able to trust his advice, I would stroke my ball and watch in shock as it turned uphill, away from the hole. In northern Europe, and Britain in particular, greens don't really have grain. There's not as much sun so growth isn't as rapid and, of much greater significance, the turf is totally different.

In America, however, grain is common, in the south on Bermudagrass greens, although clubs rotate mowing patterns so no single pattern is ever truly established. And when you hear TV commentators mention grain at a PGA Tour event put your hands over your ears and shout 'I can't hear you', because when the green is mowed as short as it is at big-time golf events, it is too short for grain to have any effect.

MASTERS TICKETS

When Dorothy and friends emerge from the forest towards the end of their arduous journey along the Yellow Brick Road and catch sight of the Emerald City, they halt and gaze upon it in wonderment. 'It's beautiful, isn't it?' Dorothy gushes. 'Just like I knew it would be!'

Most people watching the Masters from Augusta National for the first time know exactly how Dorothy feels. I first saw it in 1985 and can remember gawping at the screen for several seconds trying to take it all in. To a British lad whose few experiences of golf to that point had involved bone-chilling rain, muddy fairways and dodgy greens, Augusta's lush acres looked almost surreal. It was simply too sublime for words.

I vowed to go there one day, ideally as a player, but if necessary in the role of caddie, reporter, waiter, greenkeeper or patron (at Augusta, spectators are not referred to as fans and together they do not form a crowd: they are patrons, and many patrons make a gallery); anything if it meant getting to see this fantasyland.

I've still to make my Masters debut, more's the pity. And now, nearing 40 with my best playing days so far behind me I can barely remember them, my chances of being invited to join the rather select field are fading somewhat. And given my woeful lack of stamina, I doubt I'll ever carry a 50lb bag up and down its taxing slopes either.

I thought I might make it as a reporter a few years back, but at the last minute my editor decided he was going instead. Now, as a humble, lowly freelancer, I'm more likely to see the inside of the Queen's handbag.

Professionally (can you imagine being paid to do your job at Augusta National!) that leaves greenkeeping and waiting tables. I've mown the lawn a few times and pulled my share of pints but, in the words of Homer Simpson, I suspect this particular employer wants people 'that are good'.

So as a patron it is then. But the club's waiting list for tournament-day tickets which first opened in 1972, closed for a second time a few

Can there be a more beautiful hole than the 12th at Augusta? If I ever make it to the Masters, this is where you'll find me.

years ago. Thus, getting tickets directly from the club is not happening any time soon. Some patrons do sell their badges to brokers, but these brokers certainly know their value so don't expect to find one for much less than $900.

PRACTICE ROUNDS
With so few tournament-day tickets available, your best chance of getting inside Augusta during the Masters might be for a practice round. I'll take it because, frankly, I prefer practice days. The players are more relaxed, play more shots, hit balls on the range a bit longer, seem more willing to sign autographs, it's cheaper and you still get to see the whole course. Plus I'd rather watch the actual tournament on TV because you're far less likely to miss anything important.

✦ To get tickets direct from the club at face value, visit the official Masters website ticket information page (http://masters.org/en_US/about/ticket.html) and follow the instructions.
✦ You'll find a number of reputable brokers on the internet (just google 'Masters tickets') selling tickets for Monday at about $200. The price usually goes up to about $300 for Tuesday and $400 for Wednesday, the day of the par-3 tournament.
✦ Your last chance may be a tout, or scalper. They are legal in the state of Georgia, but must be licensed and at least 1,500ft from the entrance to the venue.

 # SUNSCREEN

You might not think it necessary in rainy old Britain, but the summer sun can get quite potent; and if you're lucky enough to play your golf in, say, Arizona or the Med, you're definitely going to need some.

Cancer Research UK estimates the number of people in the United Kingdom who develop skin cancer every year at 70,000 of which roughly 5,000 are golfers. Common sense is a great weapon in the fight against it (complete most of your round before 11am or start after 3pm if possible), but if you don't have any, remember to:

✦ Wear tightly woven fabrics, a wide-brimmed hat which shades the face, neck and ears, and golf-specific sunglasses that protect the eyes against cataracts and macular degeneration.
✦ Protect lips with a lip-balm that has an SPF of at least 15.
✦ Use only 'broad spectrum' sunscreens (they block out both UVA and UVB rays) with an SPF of at least 15. SPF 30 sunscreens usually cost way more but give only 3 per cent added protection. Apply generously 15–20 minutes before going outside and again at the turn.
✦ Sand and water reflect UV rays so keep it in the fairway.

THE DRIVING RANGE

For me, the driving range is not so much a place to practise as a bolthole; somewhere I can exit the chaotic world of work, child-rearing and home improvements and enjoy some 'alone time' – just me, my Cleveland TA-7s and a big, muddy field.

I don't go nearly enough. But when I do, I feel like I've returned to the world of my early 20s when things like trajectory and swingplane were really important. Here, my mind is not consumed with house or college payments, but five-yard draws and distance control.

JUST HOW BENEFICIAL IS IT?

Two buckets of balls is probably better for your game than two buckets of fried chicken, but it's important to realize that conditions at most ranges with artificial turf mats do not accurately reflect those you face on the course. Strike a typical mat a couple of inches behind the ball and the club skids off the surface into the ball. Thus, a swing that would most likely have caused you to hit the ball fat will probably hit it thin and you'll get a more satisfactory result, or at least, a very different result to the one you would have got playing off grass.

Better mats with silicone gel inserts (which not only give better feedback but also do a good job of preventing golfer's elbow, carpel tunnel syndrome and other wrist and forearm injuries) are on the way. But they're not cheap, so don't hold your breath waiting for them at your local range.

In addition, range balls are, by and large, completely rubbish. Hollow, hard as nails or made entirely of rubber with small chunks missing, they don't fly nearly as far as your Titleists, nor as consistently.

USE YOUR TIME EFFECTIVELY

Though great entertainment, hitting your driver as hard as you can with no specific target is worse than useless. Work on what you learned at a recent lesson instead, without cutting corners. Carry out your pro's instructions to the letter and you should see some rapid improvements. Always, always, always hit at a target and focus on the fundamentals of grip, posture, ball position and alignment. Do not treat it as an aerobic workout by whizzing through a hundred shots in ten minutes. Take your time and think about every shot as if you were playing it in competition.

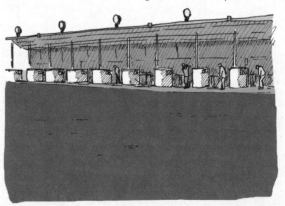

A golfer's home away from home.

THE DRINKS CART

It seems strange to me, because every golfer I know likes a snack every few holes, but I've never seen a drinks cart anywhere other than the States.

The first time most non-American golfers are confronted by the American drinks cart they are often bowled over and spend a good five minutes rummaging through all the cabinets, cupboards, refrigerators and trays trying to decide what to buy.

For me, early morning tee-times (few) usually mean coffee and a muffin. Playing around lunchtime (far more often unless it's too hot) calls for beer and a sandwich. Any other time, I'll probably have a chocolate bar, an apple and who knows, maybe even a sneaky Bushmills.

As for tipping, remember if you are on an American resort course your fellow golfers will probably be fairly affluent. So don't waste time working out what 10 or 15 per cent of $10.34 is; just hand the attendant an extra $5 and move on.

HOW TO WATCH A TOURNAMENT ON TV

Set the channel and hide the remote; you need to be prepared to make the most of a major championship on TV.

For me the experience starts a few days before the event with a good read of all the newspaper previews. I'll rip an illustrated course map out of one of the magazines, and load my fridge with drinks and snacks. There's no need for the remote control as the channel remains unchanged, but I might pull the easy chair a little closer to the television.

Now resident in the US, I have a friend round for a 'British Open Breakfast' at 6am on the morning of the fourth round. Whatever he thinks of a full English breakfast, it's all about ritual: making your preparations; the buzz of anticipation; and, best of all, watching the action unfold.

Four days of Open Championship coverage, plus preview shows and highlights. It's what TV was invented for.

DEALING WITH A SLICE

You golf therefore you slice. I'm not sure I could ever enjoy the game if I knew beyond any doubt that the next shot I was going to hit would curve viciously and uncontrollably to the right, and the one after that, and the one... Good job you can deal with it fairly easily. It'll take some effort, mind.

A slice is that oh-so-predictable shot that drives golfers absolutely nuts. A simple grip change helped me (see page 19) but that's not to say my banana shot doesn't re-appear from time to time. Now I know why it happens though, and what I have to do to put it right, or should I say left.

FIXES

We know that left-to-right sidespin, or clockwise spin, is caused by a clubhead cutting across the ball – making a glancing blow – with a face that's open relative to the path of the clubhead. The more glancing the blow, the more spin is imparted. The wickedest of all slices therefore occurs when the clubhead approaches impact on an out-to-in path with a face that's open in relation to that path.

There are dozens of swingpath fixes for you to try, but the simplest and most effective drill I know for being rid of the over-the-top move every slicer is guilty of is simply to place two balls on either side of the one you're hitting. The three balls should form a diagonal line going from low left to high right (as shown). You can only avoid the outer balls and strike the middle ball solidly with an in-to-out swing path. It's helpful when using the swingpath drill to start with small, slow swings and build up gradually to a full swing.

There are also many plausible reasons for your clubface being open at the point

of impact, but I think it safer to focus on just three; too weak a grip, too tight a grip and improper forearm rotation. And since improper forearm rotation is caused primarily by too tight or too weak a grip, let's concentrate on... grip.

First, let's make sure your grip is neutral or, better still, a touch strong. A good way to know how weak or strong your grip is, is to count the number of knuckles you see on each hand as you look down. If you have a weak grip you

With an out-to-in swingpath you'll probably clatter all three balls. Only with an in-to-out swing can you hit the middle ball alone.

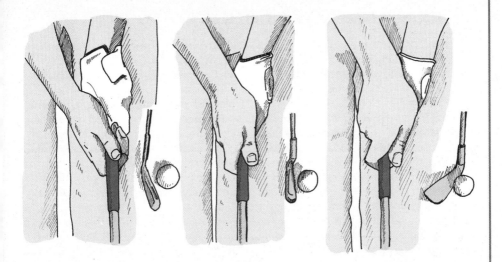

The grip in the middle is ideal, but the amateur golfer will generally do much better with a strong grip (shown left) than a weak grip (right).

can see only one knuckle of your left (top) hand and are probably hitting weak slices. Move that hand clockwise so you can see three or all four. Conversely, you may be able to see two or three knuckles on your right hand. You need to move it clockwise again so that only one is visible.

If you think the tight grip you have now is correct, holding it with the correct amount of pressure is going to feel very loose; but just try it. See how it eases tension in your forearms and shoulders? In fact, do you feel how it relaxes the whole body? Now you can really swing the clubhead (see pages 26–7), whip those hands, wrists and forearms through impact, and get a much better feel for where the clubhead is and where the face is pointing.

It is also worth remembering that a clubhead with a little offset will definitely help you trim your slice. A club is offset when the face is set back from the neck (hosel). The greater the offset, the easier it is for the slicer to square the clubface in time for impact.

It is very important to be able to feel the clubhead. People who use clubs that are too light tend to hit weak slices, or block fades because they have no feeling for where the clubhead is and can't instinctively rotate the forearms sufficiently to square the face.

Finally, remember that the harder you hit the ball with a clubface that isn't square, the more sidespin you'll impart. So if you really are having a hard time squaring the face, take a club or two more than you think you need and swing with a slightly slower tempo.

PRACTICE MAKES BIRDIE PUTTS

It's often said that a good putter is a match for anyone, which is true unless he or she takes eight to reach the green. With this in mind, it's well worth practising your putting, and using a few drills to make it a bit more enjoyable.

LONG PUTTS

Any time you're 20ft or more from the hole, the speed of the putt becomes your primary focus. Many people three-putt from this range because they leave their first effort a long way short or drill it several feet past the hole, even though their line is usually pretty good, never more than a foot or so either side of the hole. By focusing on speed, you should therefore guarantee leaving your first putt within tap-in range of the hole.

The dustbin-lid drill simply involves imagining that the hole is the size of a dustbin lid. It's an oldie and most golfers will be familiar with it, but I make no apology for including it here because it works. If your lid is anything like mine – about three feet in diameter – and your lag putt finishes within its circumference, you should have little trouble with your next putt.

Another good trick for improving your long putting is to putt balls from a variety of distances. Putt towards the edge of the putting green, attempting to bring the ball to a stop as close to the edge as possible. This is another simple but effective drill you've probably come across before, but have you actually tried it? I mean really tried it? Commit half an hour to it once or twice a week and you are almost certain to develop a better feel for speed.

SHORT PUTTS

The only time that missing a three-foot putt isn't infuriating is when it's for a 12.

You can, and will, become a much more potent golfer if you can make sure you never miss from three feet.

The stroke for long putts may bring the putter inside the target line on the backstroke, but for short putts it should move straight back and through. A really good way to develop this movement is to create a corridor of tees (below) behind and in front of your ball that prevents the putterhead from moving on the wrong path.

A final, if potentially infuriating drill is to try to hole 100 consecutive putts, from just a couple of feet. If you miss then you have to start again, whether it was your first putt or your last. This should help you keep your concentration on the greens around the course. To break the monotony, move around the hole taking no more than five putts from the same spot at any one time.

Putting down a corridor of tees. Tiger uses it a lot, and he's the best short putter who ever played the game.

Imagining a hole this size works wonders for you confidence. Aim to get long putts inside a larger target and you'll hole one every now and again.

MASTERING THE CHIP

This is a shot you've just got to have. You simply cannot get by without it. Failing to get up and down from just off the putting surface can really hurt your score and turn what should have been a great round into a distinctly average one.

Amateurs miss a lot of greens. Miss them by a lot and a solid pitch shot might be needed. But often you'll miss the putting surface by just a few yards and have a clear line to the hole. At times like these, let the standard chip-and-run come to your rescue. But, before we start, what's the difference between a chip shot and a pitch shot? Basically, a chip shot is shorter, lower and more apt to run rather than spin to a quick stop.

The chip is usually played from just off the green and from a lie that doesn't require a lot of chopping with a sand or lob wedge. The best results are achieved when your ball lands on the green as early as possible and runs like a putt the rest of the way to the hole.

BASIC TECHNIQUE
It really couldn't be simpler but, like all shots, you'll only improve with practice. Experiment a little to see how hard you need to hit the ball, how it reacts from

different lies, how the conditions of the green affect the roll of the ball, and what trajectory suits the demands of the shot.

+ From a good lie to the side of the green, and with nothing between you and the hole 20 yards away try a 6-iron, 7-iron or 8-iron.
+ Read the green as you would a putt and pick a spot where you want the ball to land.
+ Play the ball slightly back of centre and lean forward slightly (a little more weight on your front foot than back).
+ Your hands should be ahead of the clubhead at address and that is where they must be at impact. This really is of paramount importance, and it means the swing is generated mainly in the shoulders with only a little wrist action. Don't let your shoulders, arms and wrists become wooden, as you'll lose all feel, but grip the club lightly and allow for a slight wrist hinge if

I

Take a narrow, open stance, with your hands and weight slightly ahead of the ball.

2

Make a simple up and down movement of the shoulders, with perhaps a slight flex of the wrists.

the distance of the shot requires it – absolutely no scooping with the bottom hand though.

+ The ball should fly quite low. Aim for it to land on the green early and run to the hole.

CHIPPING DRILLS

Here are two of my favourite drills:

To ensure absolutely no scooping with the bottom hand, place a ball a few inches behind the ball you're hitting (to the right as you look down). Now just hit shots trying to avoid the back ball. Soon you will develop the downward strike required and make crisp, clean contact.

To develop good distance control, place four or five clubs on the ground about five feet apart, like rungs on a ladder. Hit shots with different clubs trying to land the ball between the spaces, then try it with the same club. You will learn the different trajectories you get with each club and how the ball reacts once it lands (the lower the trajectory the more it will run). Do this often enough and you will develop a feeling for which club is required to hit the chip shot you face.

3

Make a downward strike on the ball, crisp contact, a little run... and you just saved your par.

GOLFING MATTERS

Smell the Flowers (Just Do It Quickly)

It was the one and only Walter Hagen who encouraged golfers not to hurry, not to worry and, because we're here only for a short time, to smell the flowers along the way.

And I couldn't agree more – just as long as we don't hold up a group on the tee while sniffing the rhododendrons at the side of the fairway. After all, what is the use of being surrounded by all that nature if you're not going to stop and have a look at it every so often? No other sport allows participants to spend so much time amongst the flora and fauna while not actually performing.

To be honest, I'm not a huge fan of flowers on golf courses. They're okay in their place and Augusta National's look very nice, but I prefer the gorse and heather of links and heathland courses. There's nothing better than gorse when it is giving off its sweet almond aroma.

BEATING THE BUNKERS

In its rightful place, on the shores of a turquoise ocean, sand is great; however, the moment you put it in a big hole in the ground next to the putting surface it becomes bad, very bad. Pros may not regard greenside bunkers as hazards any more, but they still put the fear of God into amateurs; however, there's no need to worry, there are solutions...

If you don't like bunkers now, you should have been around in the old days when the sand was never raked. You should have played in the 1953 and 1962 US Opens at Oakmont CC in Pennsylvania when special rakes were used to create deep furrows from which creating backspin was almost impossible. You should have played before clubs everywhere decided to make the sand in their bunkers of uniform depth and texture. You should have been around when bunker play was really difficult!

Players who grumble at inconsistencies in bunkers today don't know they're born. Strong? Maybe, but bunkers are supposed to be hazards. You're supposed to be penalized for finding one. Unless you're gifted at sand play, you're meant to lose a stroke. So, instead of moaning about how the sand in this bunker is a little firmer

Hit the sand an inch or two behind the ball, depending on how firm it is.

than the sand in that last one, perhaps you should make more of an effort to avoid them in the first place. That to one side, let's assume you've found the sand, and get onto the important work of getting the ball out.

SIMPLE GREENSIDE EXPLOSION

There are two important don'ts to remember here: first, don't try to clip your ball off the sand without moving a single grain; second, don't take a ton of sand hoping your ball will be in there somewhere. So here's what you do:

+ Aim your feet and body a little to the left of your target.
+ Open the face of your sand wedge (many players actually prefer to play out of the sand with a lob wedge), then grip the club normally (do not grip the club then open the face). This puts extra loft on the club helping you get the ball out quickly.
+ Play the ball a little forward of centre (do not allow the club to touch the sand at address as this results in a two-shot penalty) and flex your knees quite a bit.
+ Visualize a spot in the sand about an inch or two behind your ball.
+ Make a fairly normal swing with perhaps a little more wrist action than normal and thud into the sand at that spot behind the ball.
+ Let the clubhead come out of the sand a few inches ahead of where the ball

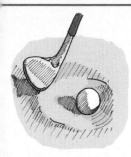

The dreaded poached egg. You won't get any backspin and you'll have far less control than you would from a good lie, but fear not; you can still get the ball out easily enough.

was, with the feeling that the clubface remains facing the sky – do not roll your wrists over.

✦ Make a full, balanced follow-through.

Right now this all probably sounds a bit complex; but follow the instructions, practise them and get used to the feeling of splashing in and out of the sand with an open clubface.

THE PLUGGED LIE

When the sand is damp, or your shot's angle of descent is almost vertical, it's likely your ball will bury itself in the sand. If you find your ball half submerged, abandon all thoughts of applying any backspin and stopping it near the hole, unless the hole happens to be on the other side of the green. From this lie, the ball will tend to run a lot so try to land it well short of the cup.

Instead of opening up your stance and the clubface as you would with a good lie, you need to square both up to the hole and push a little more weight onto your front foot. Play the ball in the centre of your stance and make a steep, aggressive swing coming down into the sand, again about an inch behind the ball.

FAIRWAY BUNKERS

Fairway bunker shots elicit a unique pitch of fear for most high handicappers.

But again, they aren't that tough if you just make a few simple alterations to your set-up:

✦ Stand square to your target.
✦ Grip down the handle of your club an inch or two.
✦ Play the ball in the middle of your stance.
✦ Make a short, compact swing and maintain your height. You shouldn't disturb too much sand.

The 60-Yard Bunker Shot

You'll often hear this is the toughest shot in the game, but by taking a pitching wedge instead of your sand iron you can actually make this shot relatively straightforward. Use a slightly open stance, a slightly open clubface, come into the sand an inch behind the ball, and there you go.

If the bunker lip is too high it may just be a sand wedge back onto the fairway. But if there is no lip, there's no reason why you can't take the club the yardage calls for, or maybe one more, and knock it on the green.

THE CLUB PRO

How the lot of most club pros has changed over the last half century. No longer do they smoke Woodbines alone in a cold back office or bow to members who regard them more as club servants.

Your club pro: smart, polite, good-humoured and incredibly hard-working.

Today's pro is not the crusty old codger of yesteryear but generally a young athlete with good business acumen whose role has shifted gradually from teacher and club repairer to entrepreneur and administrator.

Sure, the pro can still beat you with both arms tied behind someone else's back, but he's probably too busy checking his stock inventory, ordering, running club and society tournaments, managing staff, shopfitting and clubfitting to have enough time to actually play the game.

Years ago, golf pros used to play tournaments during the week and head back to their clubs at weekends to change grips, give the odd lesson and listen to members moan about the condition of the course or give them a breakdown of their round, shot by dismal shot.

The job today is certainly more invigorating than that – especially if you can swing a teaching gig in Dubai,

the States or Continental Europe – but youngsters thinking about a life in the pro-shop should ask themselves whether they can handle a working week of 80-plus hours, very few of which actually involve playing golf.

ARE YOU BEING SERVED?

My few short years as an assistant came between the thankless days of the tournament player/club pro and those of the modern incarnation with business diploma and launch monitor. In the summers, my day would start at about 7.30am, be spent mostly in the shop selling chocolate bars and cans of soft drinks, and finish whenever the last golfer went out, usually about 8pm. In the winter, my hours were cut in half and so was my pay. It was hard work for little money, but I respected my boss and was good mates with the other assistants. I loved every second.

CRAZY GOLF

Although I never quite get down on all fours to read a putt or go through my usual pre-putt routine, crazy golf is still serious business. Last summer, during a game with my three-year-old son, I actually found myself becoming a bit of a 'Competitive Dad', accusing him of serious rules infractions and considering very carefully my options at the Windmill Hole.

This particular windmill's sails rotated a little faster than I'm used to and three times I failed to get past, falling further behind my son who placed his ball one inch from the cup at the start of every hole and was thus round in a very impressive 18.

This story might seem out of place in a book about 'proper' golf, but my dad and granddad used to take me to a crazy golf course. And every time we finished, I couldn't wait to go back.

I'm not saying that crazy golf necessarily fuelled my passion for the bigger game, but it certainly didn't delay it. And, unlikely though it sounds, I may well have picked a few putting tips while negotiating a six-foot tall, orange T-Rex.

Don't even think about going round the side; that's as bad as laying up at a 450-yard par 5.

I've known several golfers who spent more time in the 19th hole than on the course.

THE 19TH HOLE

Your day at the golf course doesn't end until you've enjoyed a drink or two with your playing partners. Our time is short nowadays. When the three or four hours of recreation time you're allowed every quarter have elapsed you may need to shoot off home and do something really important like mow the lawn.

Even if it's a quick shandy, by staying on after your game you are effectively saying you enjoyed your partners' company and would like to do it again some time. By heading straight home the moment your round is over, you miss out on a fundamental part of becoming a golfer. But remember...

- Don't drink if you're driving.
- Don't start talking about your round, not with me anyway.
- Offer to buy the first round.
- Pay up on any lost bets.
- Don't push your luck. You've still got those jobs at home to do, remember?

THE GOOD PUTTER

I won't give you his name because at some point over the next 400 words or so I might get emotional and call him something I shouldn't. The guy I'm talking about had a golf swing that made your great grandmother's look powerful. But I never beat him, because with a putter in his hands he was pure gold.

The old boy might not look dangerous, but watch out. He could be deadly with a putter.

I won't tell you the name of the course, but as soon as I start writing about this demon putter, plenty of readers will instantly know who I mean, as his fame with the flat stick has spread far and wide. All I will say is that he was quite a bit older than me and couldn't hit a drive within 20 yards of mine.

The first time I played him was in the first round of a matchplay competition. On the 1st tee, he awkwardly shuffled his body into the desired position, spent at least 15 seconds getting comfortable and finally lurched the club away from the ball, which flew 200 yards tops.

After the same shuffling routine preceding his approach shot and another unconvincing strike, his ball managed to crawl up on to the edge of the green, not remotely within birdie range.

As he pulled his gruesome-looking putter from his dirty, shapeless bag – an unsightly mass of broken zips and torn pockets – he hunched over his ball in the most ungainly fashion, all the time shuffling his feet and jostling the putterhead.

As his ball rolled smoothly into the hole from 40 ft or so, I got my first indication of how this guy managed to maintain such a low single-digit handicap and how he was the current course record holder.

I was very much mistaken if I thought this first putt was a fluke because it happened again and again. He didn't birdie every hole, but he certainly had his share, and finished me off on the 14th green. I'd been guilty of judging this golfer by his appearance and wrongly interpreting his nuts-and-bolts putter and awkward style.

The fact was that he had used the same putter all his life, and performed exactly the same shuffles before every single putt he ever hit. He was totally 'in the zone' and I don't think I have ever played with or against anyone else who could putt quite like him. You have to admire it really, but at the time, boy, was it demoralizing!

THE DARK ART OF GAMESMANSHIP

Gamesmanship is the use of aggressive, often dubious, tactics such as psychological intimidation or disruption of concentration to gain an advantage over one's opponent. That's enough for many people to regard it as cheating.

However, it happens all the time and while I don't resort to it myself (I rarely play in anything of consequence any more, so what's the point?) I know that by not doing it and letting my opponent know how I feel about it, I'm simply playing into the hands of a player who does. The fact is, a cheeky remark about someone's backswing or tricking your opponent into playing the wrong club isn't breaking the rules. You may be messing with your rival's head, but it's not illegal.

Some say offenders show a shocking disregard for the game's etiquette and should therefore be disqualified (since January 1, 2004, tournament committees have been allowed to disqualify a player for a 'serious breach of etiquette') but it's difficult to prove any intent in most cases. And anyway, it's far less bothersome than someone jangling the change in their pocket, or talking loudly on their mobile phone during your backswing – both instances where disqualification is probably justified.

While I'd like to reiterate I don't really approve of gamesmanship, here are five effective moves I might employ if I were ever change my mind:

+ Hit my driver a really long way then act like I miss-hit it.
+ En route to my drive, which I know is really long, take a look at my opponent's ball as I walk by. Stop and act like it's mine then appear surprised when it's pointed out to me that in fact mine is 30 yards further on.
+ The second my opponent hits a tee shot, I would walk off the tee quickly as if it really doesn't matter where the ball ends up.
+ If my opponent walks fast, I should walk really slowly; or if my opponent is slow, I should do everything quickly. It's enough to disturb anyone's routine.
+ Any remark about your opponent's technique usually has a negative effect on their swing as they can't stop thinking about what you said. 'When did you start doing that thing with your legs/hands/head/elbows/feet?' usually works... or at least, so I'm told.

'Not my ball? Where's mine then? All the way up there? Really? Good Lord.'

🏌 THE SHANK

I remember one practice session that went something like this; warm-up, shank, shank, shank, pack up. I reckon the best way to deal with a dose of the shanks is not to deal with them at all. Just put the clubs away, go home and forget they ever happened.

The sight of the ball darting off sideways can have a profound effect on a golfer. Stunned, the brain doesn't quite know how to cope, processing a range of emotions that starts with shock and passes through embarrassment, bemusement and anger before ending with fear (am I going to do that again?), all within a couple of seconds.

Your teacher can tell you why the hosel made contact with the ball, but may not be able to explain the intangible sensation – one of golf's greatest mysteries – that makes it so difficult to regain any sort of rhythm once the darned things show up.

TECHNICAL REASONS FOR A SHANK
Some think an open clubface is to blame, others a closed clubface. I'm not sure it's the face we need to be concerned with so much as the path of the clubhead – to the inside coming back and rerouting to an extreme out-to-in path on the way down.

The golfer is usually standing too close to the ball, bending over too much or has his or her weight back on the heels at address, which causes the body to move towards the ball slightly in the downswing and thus push the club on to the out-to-in swingpath.

STOP THEM
Like I said earlier, the best plan might be to pack up and come back tomorrow. But what if you're in the middle of a round?

First, think of something else, quick! Tie your shoelaces, clean your clubs or peel a banana while remembering some good shots you've hit; and finally try these:

+ Clip the grass with a few practice swings focusing on re-establishing your tempo.
+ Stand about half an inch further from the ball.
+ Ensure your weight is on the balls of your feet.
+ Picture the toe making contact with the ball, or
+ Imagine hitting the bottom right corner of the ball.

If you can't stop shanking it in the middle of a round, try envisaging the ball divided into four quarters and aim for the one at the bottom right.

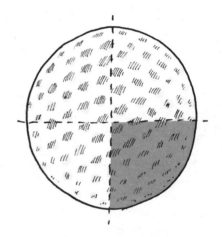

TAKING A DECENT PHOTO

Golfers take pictures of the great holes they play, or holes on which they make a miraculous birdie. Unfortunately, most of our pictures are appalling; and of the thousands I've taken on courses around the world, I'd say about four are any good.

It's easy to take a bad picture of a golf course. Take it as you're walking off the green looking backwards, or on the tee looking forwards with a lens that makes the flag on a 150-yard hole appear several miles away, and take it when the sun is high in the sky.

The great images of courses we see in books and magazines are usually the result of much forward planning. Professional photographers walk the course before shooting it to get an idea of picture-worthy holes and good locations from which to shoot them. They're up at dawn and back late in the evening when the sun is low and the light is softer – giving the hole an entirely different character to the harsh midday sun.

More often than not, they have a step ladder (or sometimes even a helicopter) to give them a bit of elevation. It's not essential, but the most memorable pictures often seem to have been taken from above the hole.

But all this is not to say that the amateur snapper can't take a perfectly decent picture with an inexpensive camera. With today's digital cameras you can shoot as many images as you like, discarding the ones that don't work and keeping those that do – all without spending a single penny. So go ahead, take hundreds – without holding up play of course – the more pictures you take the quicker you'll realize what clearly doesn't work and what might.

A bit of elevation and dramatic light bring a scene to life, you can also see how the sky fills the top third, with the tree and the pin positioned roughly on the left and right thirds.

Putting a bunker, some rough or flowers in the foreground adds interest – a great swathe of green fairway can be very dull. Avoid looking towards the sun as this risks the appearance of blotches of colour known as flare. If you really want to shoot in this direction obscure the sun behind branches or leaves. Also, while a cloudless day is better than a grey one, a few fluffy white clouds are always nice.

Finally, imagine dividing the frame into a grid of thirds. Instead of placing the subject right in the middle of the frame, where it can look pretty dull, try setting the important elements roughly on these lines of thirds. Almost invariably, this will add a bit of life to what would otherwise be a boring shot.

MAKING THE BALL BITE

Amateurs have long regarded backspin as golf's Holy Grail. The ability to hit a ball in such a way that it pitches on the green then rolls backwards marks, for many, the difference between a competent golfer and a hopeless hacker.

Every shot has some degree of backspin, just not always enough for the ball to land on the green and check up. But you don't necessarily want your ball to check anyway, as it's difficult to predict or control how far it will come back. Instead, you want it to take one hop and come to an abrupt but controlled halt, preferably close to the pin.

THE PHYSICS

There are numerous explanations for how backspin is created. Some say it's all down to a club's loft, while others claim that face grooves grip the ball. Friction generated by the downward strike of the steel face on a dimpled, rubber cover also gets a mention.

Actually, they're all correct and this combination of loft, grooves and friction explains how a motionless ball can start rotating at roughly 10,000 revolutions a minute within half a millisecond of being struck. Loft is by far the biggest contributor – the more oblique (angled) the strike, the more backspin you get – with grooves, the top edges of which grip the ball as it compresses and travels up the face, a distant second (the fact that grooveless faces perform almost as well as those with grooves in dry conditions proves how little effect the currently permitted channels have on the amount of spin produced). But while all that's incredibly interesting, the question of how you get a ball to behave like it's tied firmly to the end of a piece of string remains.

THE TECHNIQUE

There really is no great secret to it, and that's the truth. Professionals aren't magicians, nor do they have any special equipment. The clubs and balls they use are essentially the same as yours, assuming you hit a high-spinning ball such as a Titleist Pro-V1 or Nike One Platinum. (A hard, two-piece Surlyn ball like the Pinnacle Gold FX Long might be good for long-drive contests, but you'll have a job stopping it on the green unless you've got the swingspeed of Tiger Woods.) So how do they do it?

They, or rather their caddie, keep their clubs clean. Grooves affect the amount of backspin you get less than you think. But it certainly helps if you keep them clean, and you'll have a job creating backspin with a clubface like this.

They strike the ball a fraction of a second before the clubs hits the ground (see pages 22 and 41). After impact, the clubhead cuts down a little into the turf, taking a divot.

They swing fast. Sure, this is an area where the pros have an advantage but most amateur golfers possess sufficient swingspeed to create backspin. They just need to hit the ball cleanly.

You should also be aware that it is much easier to create backspin from a good lie on a firm fairway than from a less than perfect lie in long, wet grass. Satisfy all these criteria and there's no reason why your ball shouldn't behave itself on the green and settle down quickly. But like I said, you don't really want a lot of backspin no matter how cool it looks. You just want your ball to take one hop and stop.

 ## THANK YOU...

Having made only one acceptance speech in my life, and that a fair few years ago, I'm probably not as well qualified as say, Tiger Woods, to tell you what to say in your moment of victory.

However, I will say this: the safest approach is to make it instantly forgettable. After all, the only two Open Championship winners' speeches I can remember are memorable for all the wrong reasons. In 1995, John Daly accepted the Claret Jug from the secretary of the R&A, in front of the R&A clubhouse, wearing a grotesque green windshirt with his sponsor's logo slapped across the front. No one's asking you to put a blazer on John, just remove the gaudy billboard.

Then there was Nick Faldo's effort at Muirfield in 1992. After thanking the press, with whom he enjoyed a less than cordial relationship, from the heart of his bottom, he finished with an excrutiatingly regrettable rendition of 'My Way'.

Commiserate with the runner-up and thank the greenkeeper, organizers and everyone else. Then call it a day.

LAUNCH IT

I swear some people would rather hit the ball 320 yards than shoot 68. It seems strange to me, but if having your ball travel further is all important then stop slashing wildly and learn the secrets of effortless power.

First things first; your gear needs to play its part. Have your driver fitted properly. A club with the right amount of loft and correct shaft flex, plus a suitable choice of ball, will ensure optimum launch angle and low spin rate – just what we're looking for. Also, the soles of your shoes need to be clean, with the cleats in good condition. And your grips and glove (if you wear one) need to be clean and tacky. You also need to use extra-long tees.

Now soften your grip and lose any tension in your elbows and shoulders. It's natural to associate power with a tight grip, but this prevents the forearms rolling. Also, turn your right foot out so that it points to 2 o'clock rather than 12. This helps you bring the club up and down on the inside and ensures a full hip and shoulder turn which, among other things, leads to an increase in clubhead speed. Lastly, focus on maintaining good tempo and striking the ball flush.

Training

Flexibility (see pages 32–3) and strength in the abdominal area – the technical term used by many is 'core' – are all important. Your core, the engine of your swing, needs to be strong and elastic to store up and release energy quickly. A couple of good websites I visit occasionally for appropriate exercises are www.beginnertriathlete.com – which sounds a little scary, but has got a sensible and effective plan for your abs – and the mayo clinic's site at www.mayoclinic.com. Both have search tools – just type in 'core strengthening' and you should be directed to the appropriate pages. But remember to consult your doctor before starting any exercise routine.

Turning the right foot out a little lets you make a bigger hip and shoulder turn.

The right hand rolls over the left. The palm now faces behind the golfer, not up to the sky. This can only happen with a light grip and an absence of tension in the arms and shoulders. Note too the head is still behind where the ball was teed. This is a powerful release.

YOU ARE WHAT YOU EAT

Anyone tuning in to the Masters and seeing some of the plumper players waddling around might think that a good diet wasn't a particularly high priority for golfers. And for the likes of you and me it probably isn't. But that's not to say we can't all make some improvements.

I'm not suggesting anything radical here. But it would be foolish not to take advantage of research carried out into biomechanics and nutrition in recent years. A few minor modifications to your diet might not only help you feel better, it might help you play better too.

Actually, much of what the nutritionists are telling us we've known for decades; since we tore our first chunk out of a thick steak, or wolfed down our first doughnut, in fact. But the message is clear and we'd do well to remember it; large quantities of sugar and saturated fat really won't keep us in peak physical condition and allow us to perform at our best.

Take breakfast, which I think we all now know is by far the most important meal of the day. Occasionally it's a large bacon sandwich on crusty white bread with a steaming cup of coffee or tea, but most of the time it's little more than a snatched cereal bar – neither is ideal.

The former might be filling (and taste heavenly), but all that bleached flour, bacon fat and caffeine plays havoc with the metabolism raising blood sugar levels and leaving us hungry again by the time we reach the turn. Likewise, the cereal bar isn't going to satisfy our hunger for long and will result in numerous unscheduled snack breaks.

The ideal golfer's breakfast, according to a couple of well-qualified nutritionists I know, consists of oatmeal or porridge, fruit juice, yoghurt, boiled eggs and toast made with whole-wheat or multigrain bread. A nice cup of tea, ideally without sugar, is fine too. Start the day like this and you should feel pleasantly sated until the cheeseburger, fries and cola you order at the end of your round.

ON-COURSE SNACKING

According to my sources, a 180lb, or 13-stone, man should drink a litre of cool (not ice cold) water during a round of golf. And you should maintain blood sugar levels with fruit (any), snack bars (a multigrain one rather than a chocolate bar) or nuts such as walnuts, pecans, cashews and almonds. Sadly, for those of us with a taste for such things, beer and hot dogs are simply not the choice of champions.

Though my snack habits have improved of late, I don't currently have any of the above in my bag.

A ROUND WITH DAD

It may not seem like it at the time, especially when you're young and would rather be out with your friends but, apart from getting married and having kids, playing golf with your dad is just about the most special thing in the world. I wish I could still do it.

Cancer took my dad when still a relatively young man. He was first a cricketer then a golfer and he showed me how to play both. We played our first proper round of golf together shortly after my 14th birthday. I shot 101, a score that didn't really compare favourably with Seve's, the only standard that mattered, but was, Dad assured me, a pretty decent effort for a first-timer.

From then until the day he died, five years later, I guess we played only 30 more rounds together. Most of them I remember as if they happened only yesterday.

The one that really sticks in the memory though, for reasons both good and bad, was at a wonderful seaside course in Cornwall called Mullion. Perhaps I remember this particular round so well because of Mullion's fantastic location on the cliffs of the Lizard Peninsula. Or maybe it's because Dad, a solid but unspectacular 13-handicapper, played the round of his life. Or maybe I still regret the childish manner in which I reacted to being so comprehensively beaten by my old dad.

The sun was shining, the wind whipped across the hills and valleys, and white horses crashed against the rocks below. It was the sort of day courses like Mullion were built for. And while I played like a fool, Dad reeled off par after par. He finished with a very tidy 73 while I was somewhere in the mid-80s.

But instead of draping an arm round his shoulder and congratulating him on such a great round, I believe I stormed off the 18th green, locked myself in the car and opened a bag of crisps. My petulance would have impressed a Hollywood 'It' girl, but it still bothers me 20 years later. Not to worry though; I suspect the courses in Heaven look a lot like Mullion, so one day we'll have a rematch, only this time I'll beat him.

FIX A GAME WITH YOUR DAD

Working on the assumption that every 'rule' should carry with it some profound nugget of wisdom, I offer this advice; regardless of how well you get on with your father, irrespective of how good or bad at golf he is, notwithstanding the fact you haven't played with him in five years, get out for a round with your dad as soon as possible. And use the three or four hours you have together to tell him everything you've been meaning to tell him.

PROUD FATHER

One of my fondest memories of Dad is of his turning up at the award ceremony for the 1987 Haywards Heath GC Junior Club Championship, which I happened to win by seven shots!

Dad had been in hospital for weeks but his doctors thought him stable enough to come home for a few days. His first day out coincided with the tournament and, as soon as he felt comfortable, he drove up to the course to see how I'd done. Somewhere between the car park and the clubhouse, someone told him I'd shot 71 and was looking a likely winner with only two or three groups remaining.

I will never forget the smile on his face as he shook my hand (Dad was a bit Victorian and not one for hugging, backslapping or any other flagrant displays of affection). The man was virtually on death's doorstep but his joy was as evident as the disease that ravaged his body. Surgery, radiation, chemotherapy and all the rest of it had literally made him half the man he had been just a few months before, but he summoned the energy from somewhere to celebrate.

After being handed the trophy and an oversize Sony Walkman with no rewind button, I waited for the thunderous applause to die down then thanked the organizers, the greenstaff and my playing partners (see page 75). But I can't remember if I thanked my dad or not. God, I hope I did.

The golf course is the perfect place to tell your dad how much he means to you, or about how you lost your job, and just got married in Las Vegas, and how you need to borrow a couple of grand... anything really.

HOW TO HIT THE LOB SHOT

Made a lot easier in recent years by the introduction of 60° and 64° wedges, the lob rises and drops almost vertically and therefore runs very little after it lands. Phil Mickelson has perfected this spectacular shot, making an almost full backswing but hitting the ball no more than 20–30 yards.

The lob is a very useful shot to have if the hole is cut just the other side of a bunker or water hazard, where you will need to hit the ball high and limit the amount of roll.

If he were to make poor contact, Mickelson would skin the ball 100 yards over the ropes and into the shrubbery beyond. His lobs almost take his nose off, however, shooting straight up and plummeting to the ground usually no more than a foot or two from the hole.

It's very important to remember this is a difficult shot, requiring exceptional hand-eye co-ordination, and one that Mickelson attempts only when he needs to; when there is a bunker, some water, or a mound between him and the hole, and he needs to loft the ball over the trouble before stopping it quickly.

It's also worth mentioning that this shot is made a lot easier if the ball is lying on a fairly soft bit of ground. The quality of the contact needed for playing a lob off a very tight lie is beyond most club golfers – and don't even think about playing it out of a divot.

+ Assess how high the shot needs to go, how hard you need to hit it and where you want the ball to land.
+ You're probably attempting a lob because there is something nasty between you and the hole, so make sure you clear it.
+ Play the ball forward of centre, with your hands level with the ball.
+ Establish a wide, balanced base with a little more knee flex than usual. Aim left of the target.
+ Your weight should be evenly distributed between your feet.
+ Allow for just a little wrist hinge.
+ Keep your head very still and your eyes on the back of the ball.
+ Accelerate the clubhead through the ball and finish with your weight mostly on your front foot.

MAGNIFICENT MUNICIPALS

The publicly owned golf course may be a little ragged at the edges and its greens might not putt as smoothly as those at private courses. But given the price of a round, who's complaining?

Every Friday afternoon a four-ball of college students would duck out of double sociology and drive up to Tilgate Forest GC, a fantastic municipal course in the UK. There, the game of choice was usually a Texas Scramble as three of the four were total hacks who weren't welcome at any other golf facility and who didn't much fancy keeping their own scorecard.

A round at Tilgate might take these intrepid class-skippers anything from two and a half to five hours depending on who was in front of them; two and a half if the course was quiet, five if they got lumped behind a group with no clue what 'expected pace of play' meant. Most of the time it was five because Tilgate, like most municipals, was extremely busy and attracted a number of golfers for whom etiquette was something other people did.

From bad golf to bad manners, from people failing to hit their tee shot past the forward tees and having to drop their trousers, to kids running out from the bushes and nicking golf balls, it all goes on at the municipal. Here's a sample of some of the more interesting things I've witnessed:

+ A middle-aged man who hit his tee shot between his legs after predicting a gentle fade that would keep his ball short of the fairway bunkers. Everyone who saw it collapsed in stitches, except the guy who hit the shot. He looked bemused and checked his club, convinced it was somehow responsible.
+ A nervous-looking man who hit a shank off the 1st tee that went through the windscreen of a Jaguar XJS owned by one of his playing partners.
+ A young man dressed in nothing but a pair of skimpy, electric-blue shorts and a pair of sunglasses who told me to go forth and multiply before he hid his club somewhere about my person, after I had politely enquired if my group might be allowed to play through his.
+ An eight-ball that spent at least three minutes running round the green screaming and high-fiving after one of them holed a chip shot.

'Munis', you've got to love 'em.

Municipals are not known for the excellence of their greens.

HOW GREEN ARE THE GREENS?

A 2006 survey by the Scottish Golf Environment Group (SGEG) found that 51 per cent of courses applied less than 80kg of potassium fertilizer per hectare to their greens; but what does that really mean?

Rest assured these figures mean as little to me as they probably do to you. I haven't the faintest idea just how much potassium fertilizer would be considered excessive; but I do know that the question of the environment is important enough to warrant such a survey, and that courses monitor their their environmental impact closely enough to be able to answer it. Both of these facts are welcome developments from the days when some courses would unthinkingly dump bags of fertilizer on anything that grew.

The SGEG isn't alone, of course. Groups researching the impact of golf on the environment have been popping up wherever golf is played for 20 years or more. Thanks to their influence, and a growing preference among golfers for 'minimalist' courses, the world has seen a definite shift away from the over-fertilized and over-watered layouts of the 1980s and '90s.

It was these sorts of developments that gave golf a wretched reputation among environmentalists and indeed the wider public. And like its enduring reputation for bad clothing (see pages 42–3), golf has found it hard to shake its poor image despite the numerous environmentally friendly initiatives now in place around the world.

A 2002 University of London survey backs this perception up with numbers, showing that 80 per cent of the golfers surveyed believed that courses were good for the environment, while only 36 per cent of non-golfers agreed. In the States,

Golf faces some serious challenges regarding irrigation, but thankfully the days of wanton over-consumption are becoming a thing of the past.

where many courses, especially those in the south-west, use vast quantities of water every day (some courses are replacing the grass on their greens and tees with synthetic turf to cut costs) the figures are similar. Only 30 per cent of non-golfers in America say the game is beneficial to the environment.

As a golfer I suppose I'm biased, but I think that many of these negative judgements are based, at least in part, on the images of the past. Perhaps people should visit the truly organic Askernish GC on South Uist, or the wonderfully 'un-manicured' Temple GC in Berkshire, to see how far the game has progressed since the substance-abusing, hose-happy days of the 1980s. And besides, if the land is up for development anyway, would you really rather have yet another concrete shopping centre and vast car park? Sure, golf still has some way to go, but it's at least heading in the right direction.

THE GOLFING GODS

Happy to give me a birdie on the forgettable 17th, they heckle me on my backswing at tee of the heroic 18th. Capricious, fickle and frequently vindictive, the golfing gods have been having fun at my expense for 20 years.

I know the golf gods exist because I've seen things happen on golf courses that really shouldn't. I've seen balls skim across water and cosy up against the flag. I've seen balls destined for the woods ricochet off overhead power lines back on to the fairway. I've seen thinned shots hit halfway up the pin at 100 miles an hour, but drop into the hole. Yes, I've seen countless shots happen that couldn't possibly have occurred without some outside agency or other being involved.

The trouble is, however, none of these outrageous strokes of good fortune ever happen to me. The luckiest I've ever been on a golf course was when I lost control of a buggy that slid down a muddy embankment, but stopped just short of the river at the bottom.

I'm pretty sure that playing golf while believing that the game's gods have got it in for me does my game no good whatsoever. But much of the time, I can't help myself.

GOLFERS OF THE WORLD UNITE

Global golf travel has many attractions, not least of which is playing with some pretty exotic characters in some unfamiliar places.

Until you get on a plane bound for some far-flung corner of the planet, your experiences of this game will remain fairly bland – at least, not nearly as far-fetched as they could be. Some sunny resort at home or abroad is as far as many will venture, but for those with a touch of wanderlust that's just a little too predictable.

My globe-trotting days may well be behind me, at least for the time being, now that I've got a family to think about. But the memories of past trips, and the people I played with, keep me going until I can venture off once more into the unknown. Here are just a few of the weird and wonderful individuals I've met playing golf:

+ a bushman in the Outback who lived the life of Crocodile Dundee (apart from the bit where he goes to New York);
+ a student in South Africa who played bare foot, and off scratch;
+ a Hindu preacher in Indonesia;
+ a billionaire in Hong Kong;
+ the 11-time winner of Costa Rica's national championship;
+ and a Zimbabwean farmer who gripped the club with his left hand below his right, but still played to his three handicap.

GET YOURSELF FITTED

Listen very carefully, I shall say this only once: you must have your golf clubs custom-fitted to your specific body type and swing characteristics if you're ever going to fulfil your potential.

Of course it's in their interests to say this, but professional clubfitters – not the cowboys who build you a set of clubs based on their best guess – insist that poor-quality clubs that have been custom-built will work better for you than a top-quality set that hasn't. The whole point of custom-fitting is to ensure your good swings are justly rewarded, and that you no longer have to manipulate your swing to compensate for clubs that are not suited to you.

A static fit is a good start but now you need to hit balls, ideally with a launch monitor analyzing your every move.

Two Ways to Get Fitted

There are two methods for fitting a golfer: static and dynamic. A static fit can be completed at most club manufacturers' or golf retailers' websites. Your height, hand size and one or two other measurements are taken, and your current clubs' specifications and resulting ball flight assessed. The static fit is a good starting point, certainly better than no information at all, but to be fitted as comprehensively as possible you need to add a dynamic fitting. This is where a launch monitor records your swing speed, the ball's launch angle, its spin rate and the resulting carry.

Who Can Do It?

Most club professionals are certified clubfitters (manufacturers license the pro to fit their clubs). Sometimes a fitting, which normally takes up to an hour, is free, and if there is a small charge the pro will probably reimburse it if you buy the clubs from him or her.

Independent clubfitters (try the International Professional Association of Clubfitters at www.ipac.com) are usually well-qualified and affiliated with a retail facility, but don't necessarily teach or play the game for money. They perhaps give the most thorough fittings – this is, after all, what they do – and will give you a list of your specifications at the end of the session. You will have to pay a little more for this than you would a club pro, but you can then take your specs to a vendor to order the clubs.

A demo day is a really good opportunity for you to try out some new clubs.

Retail stores are a better place to have clubs custom-fitted than they were ten years ago, but they still have their limitations as the fitting tends only to be static. If they do have a launch monitor the staff are sometimes clueless as to how it actually works: 'Have you tried turning it off and on again?'

Club demo days allow you to hit new models with a wide range of specifications but usually without a launch monitor present. So you don't get a scientific evaluation of your shots – spin rate, ball speed and so on. Although for some people that stuff doesn't really matter as much as gauging how a club feels and simply seeing the results.

If you really want to push the boat out, visit the fitting studio at a manufacturer's headquarters. I went to Callaway's Performance Lab once and was blown away by the rate at which technology had clearly advanced since I was last fitted. The process was also extremely good fun; like playing a games console, only ten times better.

THE SHAFT IS ALL-IMPORTANT

If you don't think the shaft has much effect on your golf, try hitting Tiger Woods' clubs (actually, he probably wouldn't let you). If your swing is anything like mine, you wouldn't get the ball much more than 20ft off the ground, even with an 8-iron. The shafts are way too stiff for the likes of you and me and they load and unload (bend and bend back) very little or too late for the average amateur to square the clubface. Shots therefore tend to fly low and to the right. A session with a launch monitor and a decent fitter are essential if you want to identify the shaft that works best for you.

As you can see, the launch monitor processes an awful lot of information – clubhead speed, launch angle, spin rate and so on. But it can't tell you to stop wearing yellow trousers.

SOLE/FACE TAPE

A launch monitor provides information that assists the fitter in optimizing clubface loft and shaft flex. The lie of the club (the angle of the shaft to the ground at address) is another very important aspect that also needs to be considered.

If your clubs are too flat at address the shaft will naturally be more upright at impact and the toe will contact the ground with the heel raised. The shot will fly to the right of your intended target. Likewise, if your clubs are too upright you will tend to hit it left.

You can record the lie of your clubs by hitting balls off a lie board with impact tape stuck to the sole of your iron. If the resulting mark appears toward the toe, the lie is too flat; in the middle means it is just right; while near the heel means the club is too upright.

The mark left when the sole hit the lie board is in the middle of the tape, which means the owner of this club cannot blame the lie for a wayward shot.

KEEPING SCORE

Shoot a ten-under-par 62 but fail to sign your scorecard or fill it out correctly, and instead of winning the tournament you could be disqualified. So how about a few quick reminders to help you avoid that horrible situation?

We all know the story. Argentine Roberto De Vicenzo makes a three at the 71st hole at the 1968 Masters but playing partner, Tommy Aaron, puts him down for a par 4 by mistake. After finishing with what he thinks is a round of 65 that should at least earn him a berth in a play-off, it is discovered De Vicenzo has signed his card before noticing Aaron's error. The four stands and a 65 becomes a 66 – one too many for the play-off.

In the heat of battle at a major championship, with his focus elsewhere, it's almost understandable, albeit regrettable, for a player to miss slight inaccuracies such as that which De Vicenzo overlooked. But there is no excuse for you and me, after playing a comparatively insignificant club event, to get it wrong. There's no great pressure, you probably won't already be thinking about your round tomorrow, and how you're going to win the tournament and you won't be expected in the media tent for a press conference. You have plenty of time and all you have to do is make sure the score your partner has you down for on each hole matches the score you put in the 'Marker's Score' column on your partner's card (and that this score is correct of course). You don't even have to add it all up and write in the total – let the officials do that.

Filling in a scorecard is very simple, but mistakes are often made. Just ensure that the scores for each hole are correct, and that you have signed your card before handing it in.

TURN IN A CORRECT SCORECARD

It's so important that it's worth going over the basics:

+ Fill in all the info at the top of the card (your name, handicap, date, and so on).
+ Exchange cards with another member of your group.
+ Write that player's scores in 'Player's Score', yours go in 'Marker's Score'.
+ At the end of the round, make absolutely sure the numbers you have down for yourself under 'Marker's Score' are the same as those your partner wrote down on your card, under 'Player's Score'. Say the scores out loud if need be.
+ Only when the scorecards tally and you are confident everything is in order, should you sign your partner's card (under 'Marker's Signature') and give it back, then sign your own ('Player's Signature') and hand it in.

GO BACK AND START YOUNGER

For most, the golf swing does not come naturally. It's an unfamiliar action that requires great flexibility. So you want to start swinging a golf club and ingraining the movements before it's too late.

Let me rephrase that (because it's never too late to take up golf); while your body is still sufficiently pliant to perform the motion without too much pain.

Some people do pick up a club for the first time the day after retiring, thinking that a few holes in the sunshine with friends every day might be a good way to spend their twilight years. But contorting hands and limbs in a manner as yet untried, in order to propel a ball high into the air, will not come easily to an arthritic man who's had both hips replaced.

As far as I know, the only major champion who picked up a club for the first time after his 20th birthday was America's Larry Nelson who started at 21 and eagled the first hole he ever played! Exceptions like Nelson aside, you really need to start at an age when your body is supple and athletic. If you have a kid who wants to be the next Tiger Woods, take him or her to a pitch-and-putt course, a driving range or even a crazy golf course

where they can have a good time. Don't buy any equipment just yet. Let them decide they are definitely interested in golf before you go wasting your money. Then, when it's clear they really are taken with the game, take them along to a local course and introduce them to the pro. A decent pro should have experience of teaching kids and make these early experiences enjoyable. And if you live near a professional tour venue, there's no better way to fuel a kid's fascination than by taking him or her to watch their heroes.

When it's time for your kid's first set, don't just cut down your old irons, the clubheads are probably too heavy for a youngster. Invest in some proper junior clubs instead. And please, please don't push your child; let them discover for themselves what a fun, challenging and enriching game golf is. If you try to force them into it, the chances are that your son or daughter will just end up resenting it.

Find a pro who makes lessons fun. Yelling at a bunch of kids to keep their heads down is not terribly encouraging and will put them off in no time at all.

A DAY AT THE OPEN

Since the first championship was held in 1860, when just eight professionals entered, the Open has grown somewhat. A far cry from the days in which Willie Park picked up the first of his four victories, in 2007, winner Padraig Harrington beat 155 other golfers to the £750,000 top prize and the famous Claret Jug. It's a huge event and one of Britain's greatest. If you get the chance, you have to go.

I'm sure some American readers will choke on their corn dogs and spray latte through their noses when I say this; the Open Championship is the greatest tournament in the world.

Golf fans in the States (which is where I now live, so I'm expecting more than a little comeback) understandably perceive the Masters and their own national Open as being greater, but in my daydreams I'm always holing out on the 18th green at St Andrews to win by a stroke and be crowned Champion Golfer for the Year.

A day at the Open is a memorable occasion. The exhibition tent is well worth a visit and I like to spend a good hour watching players warm up at the practice ground before sitting in front of the huge TV screen in the tented village with a burger and beer. But, of course, you've got to head out to the course at some point.

I worked out long ago that trying to follow groups including Tiger Woods, Ernie Els, John Daly, or old favourites such as Seve Ballesteros and Jack Nicklaus was a total waste of time. You have to be extremely fit and get a bit lucky to see so much as half a dozen shots without standing on tip-toes and craning your neck, or having some four-year-old kid on its parent's shoulders accidentally kick you in the face.

Instead I might follow a group of lesser-known players so I can at least see the course (following a group the whole way round can mean a hike of between six and ten miles depending on how often you get lost and how many visits you make to the beer tent or toilet).

More often than not though, I'll find an empty seat among the 17,000 or so available in the grandstands and watch every player come through. There I can sit back and watch the world's best golfers playing one of the game's greatest courses for its biggest prize. Apart from the occasional fool shouting 'Go in the hole', 'You the man' or any number of equally moronic utterances, it really couldn't get much better.

When Italy's Costantino Rocca holed his monster putt on the 18th green at St Andrews in 1995 to force a play-off with John Daly, I was watching from a grandstand. As the guy sat next to me jumped up to celebrate he knocked my glasses clean off my face. By the time I located them all the commotion had died down.

THE RULES OF THE GAME

The current R&A rulebook (you can find a pdf at www.randa.org) is 208 pages long. Some of the pages are filled with ads admittedly, but we are talking about one exhaustive set of guidelines and instructions here. As it says in the foreword, the book is the result of four years' work and consultation between the R&A and USGA. It would take at least that long for me to read the thing and commit its finer points to memory.

Unbelievably there are 40 pages of decisions and definitions before you even get to Rule 1. There are 34 rules in all (28 of which have been revised for the 2008–11 edition) with all sorts of clauses and sub-clauses. There are three appendices (the first of which has three parts), ten rules on amateur status, a section on gambling and a 24-page index. Frankly, it's terrifying.

When I worked in the pro shop, I had a pretty good grasp of the rules. But now, 16 years on, I'd say I am only slightly more familiar with them than your average weekend golfer. Basic rules such as what to do when your ball is in an unplayable lie, where to drop after finding a water or lateral water hazard, and the procedure one should follow after hitting out of bounds are still etched on my mind, I suppose because I now refer to them more often than I'd like. But rules like 25-1a: 'Interference by an abnormal ground condition' just don't roll off the tongue quite as easily as they once did.

I won't go into details about any specific rules, for that I would recommend *Golf*

Rules of Golf

You've got the weekend to learn it. There will questions...

Rules Explained by Peter Dobereiner and Bill Elliott, or the light-hearted *Do I get a Drop?* by Doug Anderson. Instead I thought it might be more fun to tell you the story of the respected club veteran who I saw break the rules many times in a single round.

He had been at the club for decades, was one of 'the boys' and may even have been on a committee or two. At the 18th, his drive came to rest a few feet in front of a tree. His backswing was impeded and in trying to advance the ball, he missed it altogether. Quickly, all in one non-stop motion in fact, he took another swipe and got his ball up near the green. After a chip and a putt he was in for five. When we came to signing our cards, however, he queried the five, saying he had made a par 4. 'But didn't you...' I stopped abruptly; a junior accusing one of the most respected men in the club of cheating would not go down well.

I bring this up because, despite the fact it happened 21 years ago, I can still see him, clear as crystal, chopping twice at his ball by the tree. Cheating stinks and the stench never goes away.

PLAYING WITH THE PROS

If you're fortunate enough to play in a pro-am you need to know the drill in order to avoid upsetting your pro, and looking a total berk.

Ionce played in a pro-am with a well-known Australian player. My four partners and I had chosen him at a draw party the previous evening hoping that not only would he give us a few great tips, but also foster a fun and relaxed atmosphere with the genial, easy-going manner of your typical Aussie.

He didn't say a word for eight holes. As invited guests, we hadn't paid a penny for the privilege of being there, but let me tell you, I for one was beginning to feel a little hard done by.

An amusing incident on the 9th tee, which will have to wait for another day I'm afraid, and another on the 13th cracked the ice, however, and by the 18th we were all getting along famously.

Curious why 'Our Pro' had blanked us for eight holes I asked his caddy if there had been a problem. 'You should see some of the morons we get,' he said. 'He doesn't really enjoy these things, because even though we're working he's expected to laugh at every lame joke and offer advice all the time. It just took him nine holes to realize you lot were okay.'

'Our Pro' was, of course, no different from the vast majority of the other pros with whom you could one day be paired. So despite shelling out big bucks, and therefore having every right to expect your pro to join in the fun, remember this is the last practice round before the tournament starts; they might not be the life and soul of the five-ball.

Your pro is already in the hole for three, so what on earth are you doing lining up a putt for a seven?

TIPS FOR PRO-AM PARTICIPANTS

It's mostly common sense really, but here are a few pointers to help you get the most out of your encounter with a pro.

+ Look smart and show up on the tee five minutes before the pro.
+ Greet the pro with a hand shake and a smile. By all means say what a pleasure it is to meet him or her, but nothing too gushing, mind.
+ For goodness sake don't worry about how badly you play. I guarantee you, the pro has seen worse.
+ Unless you really are a stand-up comedian, do not act like one.
+ Once your pro has made a birdie and you have no way of improving on that, you must pick your ball up.

PLAYING WITH THE BOSS

When it comes to playing with the boss protocol is far stricter in the States than the UK, for example; but wherever you are playing in the world, it's worth having a think about what you and your boss can expect from the day.

Imagine you're an office junior and have just received an invitation to play golf with your CEO, the infamous Gordon Gekko. You've only ever seen him twice, certainly never spoken to him and now you have an invite – issued by his PA of course – to spend four hours in his company. He's an intimidating man and you're anxious about making a good impression as you realize this round could make or break your career.

You prepare the night before, choosing your outfit carefully and cleaning your clubs and shoes. You arrive at the course well ahead of time and are either warming up on the range as Mr Gekko arrives or sitting in the lounge with his favourite tipple waiting for him. On-course dialogue is entirely at his discretion, but however it goes, it never gets chummy.

Do you beat him? No hard and fast rules on that. You decide to gauge his demeanour, asking yourself how he'd react if you took him to the cleaners. Would he be impressed or find it disrespectful and make your life a living hell?

Although Gekko is a work of fiction and didn't play golf (racquetball was his game), this type of scenario isn't uncommon in the States, where frequent magazine articles spell out exactly what's expected of the employee.

PLAYING FOR REAL

In my experience, workers needn't be quite so apprehensive or pay quite as much attention to the details. That said, your boss won't be terribly impressed

if you disregard the preferred code of behaviour altogether. So it can't hurt to:

+ Turn up before your boss.
+ Look presentable.
+ Remember that your boss isn't your best mate. Keep the language as clean as your shoes, and for that matter make sure your shoes are clean.
+ Silence your mobile phone.
+ Try hard to win without being unpleasantly competitive.
+ Offer to pay for everything. Your boss probably won't accept your offer, but it doesn't mean it isn't appreciated.

My friend John, a marketing executive, concurs with the above, but adds he would book a lesson for a few days before the round. He'd then have a bit of time to practise what he learned.

Unless you know your boss very well, keep the banter clean and don't talk about the office unless your boss brings it up.

HOW TO CURVE THE BALL... INTENTIONALLY

Shaping shots to the left or right is a dying art. That's not to say today's golfers can't do it, they just don't need to very often.

Golf shots fly straighter today than they used to, not necessarily because today's golfers are any better than the golfers of the 1960s say (they aren't), but because today's equipment is. Low-spinning golf balls and light titanium drivers, in which manufacturers can add or remove weight to specific areas of the clubhead to affect a certain type of shot, have seen a reduction in the amount of sidespin that a golfer can create.

That's no bad thing when you're faced with a narrow, tree-lined par 4 where you must find the fairway. But because pulls and pushes – affected by the golfer's swingpath not the ball's specifications – still happen every bit as often as they used to, what do you do when you miss the fairway, get stuck behind a tree and need to curl one round the branches to find the green?

While unintentional side-spin is less of a problem than it used to be, golfers needing to hook or slice a shot on purpose can still do it with a few alterations to their set-up and, in the case of a hook, some quick wrists or, for a slice, quiet wrists that prevent the release of the clubhead.

THE INTENTIONAL DRAW/HOOK

The laws that determine the flight of a golf ball (see page 28) tell us that a hook – a shot that starts to the right of your target and curves back to the left – occurs when the clubface is closed in relation to that swingpath. So, to hit a big, slinging hook round a tree, align your feet, hips and shoulders well to the

right of it but the clubface at the target. The clubface is now closed in relation to your stance and should therefore be closed to the path of your swing. Now, when you swing back normally along the line of your feet and hit the ball with this closed clubface the ball will miss the tree to the right and hook back towards your target. At least that's the theory.

✦ To encourage more hook spin, feel like your wrists are rolling over through impact, and the toe of the clubhead beats the heel back to the ball. Feel

Target line

Aim to the right of the target

To hit a big hook, aim your body well to the right of your target, but the clubface at it. Your aim lines converge. And roll the wrists a little more than usual.

like the inside of your left forearm and the top of your right forearm face the sky. The feeling is not unlike a top-spin forehand in tennis (admittedly just with the right hand).

✦ The more you want to hook the ball, the further right of the target you aim your body and the more you roll the wrists. So, if you just need a small draw, keep the clubface looking at the target but aim your body only slightly to the right. As always, grip the club lightly.

The Intentional Fade/Slice

If you missed the fairway to the right, chances are you'll have to hit a big slice that starts well to the left of the trees then cuts back towards your target. By now you've probably worked out that to hit this slice you do the opposite to what you would when hitting a hook, but just in case:

✦ Aim your feet, hips and shoulders well to the left of the obstacle.
✦ Aim the clubhead at the target.
✦ Swing along the line of your feet and hold off the release of the clubhead. The heel of the clubhead must beat the toe to the ball. Feel like your forearms remain well separated.
✦ The more slice-spin you want, the more your aim lines (clubface and body) should diverge.

Just Feel It

At a clinic several years ago, I asked Welshman Ian Woosnam how he hit such a delightful little draw. He thought about it for a few seconds. 'Er, I don't

Keep your clubface facing the target for a fade but aim your body well left. Your aim lines diverge. Hold off the release a little.

really know to be honest,' he replied. 'I just do.' At a similar event with Colin Montgomerie a few years later, I asked the big Scot how he managed to hit his powerful fade time and time again. He didn't really know either.

The lesson is that both Woosnam and Montgomerie are 'feel' players. They just feel the shot they need to play. Montgomerie said he didn't set up any differently for a fade than he would do for the very occasional draw that he hit, but that if he did mean to hit a draw he probably felt his hands and wrists needed to be a little bit more active through the ball.

YOUR PRE-SHOT ROUTINE

Humans often perform certain actions better if we aren't conscious of what we're doing. Whatever the sport, the best players are able to exist in an unthinking moment, putting everything into motion without the distractions of the mind.

After practising for months and months, Olympic figure skaters execute their routines not by desperately trying to remember the difference between a double axel and a triple salchow, but by simply allowing their mind and body do what they have been trained to do. Likewise, golfers swing at their free-flowing, rhythmical best when they minimize conscious thought and let the subconscious take over.

A pre-shot routine is a very good way to do this, and you'll notice every single professional golfer bar none has one and carries it out for every single shot they play. By enacting exactly the same routine every time we can remove unhelpful technical clutter from our heads and arrive at the ball tension-free and able to swing the club with the freedom, balance and speed of which we are capable.

UNIVERSAL ELEMENTS
Your routine can include whatever movements and actions you like. But remember; it will only be any good if you repeat exactly the same movements before every shot.

Having selected a club and decided what sort of shot to play, a typical pro will stand a few yards behind the ball, picking a target and picturing a good result. Then he or she will move alongside the ball and align the clubface before moving into position. Once in position, the pro eases the tension in the forearms by lightening the grip and waggling the club. Then the initial move away from the ball is smooth and fluid rather than jerky and erratic.

A routine such as this will help switch off your mind, and promote a fluid swing, stopping the demons in your head from distracting you at the top of your swing with thoughts of what went wrong the last time you played this hole.

Your routine must be the same for every shot. Try aligning the clubface to the target first, then your body in response to the clubface. And waggle the club, shuffle your feet, flex your knees, anything, to avoid getting 'stuck' over the ball.

ETIQUETTE

Call me a joy-killing, party-pooping, sport-spoiling wet blanket, but part of the reason our sport is so special is because we have a set of behavioural guidelines that the vast majority of players actually adhere to.

This is not some pointless code; without it, the condition of our courses would suffer, and playing golf would not be so safe and enjoyable... and these days a serious breach of etiquette could result in disqualification from a competition.

+ Most important is a regard for other players' safety. Never hit until the group in front of you is well out of range. Don't make practice swings close to other players, and if there is even the slightest possibility your ball will hit another player then shout 'Fore'.
+ It doesn't matter how badly you want to win, you should show your playing partners respect by standing well away from them as they play their shots; ensuring your mobile phone is silenced; not walking on or casting a shadow over their putting lines, or standing directly behind the hole while they are putting. And after you've putted out,

Ask your playing partners if they would like you to tend the flag.

Repair pitch marks by inserting your repair tool at the back of the mark and pushing the turf towards its centre. Tap down gently with your putter. Do not lever turf up to fill the dent, or twist the repair tool.

stick around until your partners have finished; don't rush off to the next tee.

+ Your group should keep pace with the group ahead; or if a gap opens up between you and those in front, and the group behind catches up, you should invite them to play through. Maintain your pace by being ready to play when it's your turn; placing your bag so you don't have to walk to the front of the green after finishing; and walking briskly, filling in your scorecard as you go. Also, if your ball may be lost, play a provisional and call the group behind through as you look for the original.
+ Finally, look after the course: be careful not to take divots with practice swings; replace your divots, rake bunkers; repair pitch marks; don't stand your bag on the green or too close to the teeing area; and remove and replace the flag carefully.

EYE-BALLING

Back when there were no yardage charts, laser rangefinders or digital GPS-enabled distance-measuring devices, golfers used to estimate the distance left to the hole with, imagine this, their own two eyes.

Despite the relentless advance of technology there's a lot to be said for relying on your eyes today. For a start, standing at your ball, looking at the flag and deciding that it's roughly 147 yards away is an awful lot cheaper than doing it with any of the latest gadgets, or for that matter a yardage planner booklet, which are becoming ever more expensive.

The advantage of using hi-tech instruments to measure your yardage is of course superior accuracy. I don't care how long you've been eye-balling, a gadget that picks up high-frequency, low-power radio signals from four GPS satellites orbiting the Earth and deduces its own position and then the flag's using a mathematical principle called trilateration is probably going to beat your best guess, at least more often than not. As far as I can see, that's where the benefits end, however. There is an argument, which the manufacturers push relentlessly, that says such gadgets and gizmos speed up play, but I'm not convinced. They'll certainly lop a chunk of time off your round if you're in the habit of pacing out the yardage to the hole on every shot, but who does that?

If, however, you are in the market for one of these things, then consider some of a GPS system's advantages over a rangefinder:

+ A funky colour screen.
+ You can input all your stats, keeping tabs on your strengths and weaknesses.

+ You will know your exact elapsed playing time (although you could do this with your watch).
+ You can measure your shots and know the distance you hit each club enabling the device to recommend clubs.
+ You do not need a direct line of sight to the hole to know the distance remaining.
+ The initial purchase can be cheaper than for a rangefinder.
+ They are often lighter and usually less bulky than rangefinders.
+ They are quicker than a rangefinder. Just look at the screen and pick your club.

You can't order pizza with it but it gives pretty accurate yardages.

But, of course, the laser rangefinder has its advantages too:

+ No annual subscription fees.
+ No downloading course information from manufacturer's database.
+ Provided you can keep your hand still, it can actually be more accurate.

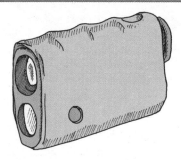

There is an enormous range of rangefinders on the market.

The choice between GPS and laser is not cut and dried. Each has its advocates, and there are decent arguments in favour of both. Myself, I'm staying out of it. My eyes (well, if I'm honest my contact lenses) still work well enough for me to know it's an 8-iron.

GPS units and laser rangefinders can tell you the shot is 134 yards, not the 130 you estimated. But for how many of us does that really make a difference to the club we choose and the type of shot we play?

 HATS OFF

On a top shelf in the darkest corner of my closet are 63 baseball caps I've bought, been given, or picked up on various golf trips. Some of them are so gaudy it's unlikely they'll ever see the light of day, but there are a handful that get an airing once every so often.

Thanks to Tiger Woods' choice of headwear, the baseball cap is now very much part of the golfer's uniform. Shallow-fronted and narrow-brimmed is the style of choice for most of today's young studs, but among the sport's older participants you still see the odd over-size front, mesh back and wide brim; a style that should, in my opinion, be accompanied by a piece of straw dangling from the golfer's mouth.

Other acceptable styles, albeit ones that only certain individuals might be able to pull off, include; the pork-pie hat, bucket hat, flat cap, coconut hat, ivy cap, army hat, the fleece cap and even the visor, whose popularity I have never really been able to understand.

Hats that I don't much care for, besides the aforementioned visor, include Panamas and those circular-brimmed straw hats that Greg Norman used to wear. The only person for whom that design ever looked good was Greg Norman, and then only just.

THE YIPS AND HOW TO SHAKE THEM

What a miserable existence it would be knowing that no matter how brilliant your drive and approach shots were, you were still going to double-bogey the hole after making four involuntary stabs at the ball with your putter. To everyone with the yips; my heart goes out to you.

Most people my age associate the yips with Bernhard Langer, the incredible German professional who has overcome them a number of times with a series of different putters and grips, not to mention perseverance and hard work. One of the earliest reported cases, however, was six-time Open champion Harry Vardon who would address the ball and 'watch for the right hand to jump'.

For years it was assumed the problem was purely psychological. But recent research has identified another culprit. Not only are fear and performance anxiety (what most golfers term 'choking') to blame but also focal dystonia, a neurological disorder often described as an occupational cramp and characterized by involuntary movements or spasms. Fine, but how does this new-found knowledge help you get rid of the darn things?

YIPS TIPS
Considering how many websites, magazine articles and books are devoted to the subject, my paltry suggestions on how to get rid of the yips might seem a tad simplistic, but here goes:

✦ You need to stop worrying so much. No 17-handicapper should get the yips. What's the worst that can happen if you miss a few putts – you'll become an 18-handicapper?

✦ You've got to try something different than what you've been doing for so long. Try a new grip, a belly or broomhandle putter, or putt left-handed. Try a new grip on a left-handed broomhandle – you get the point; do something unusual.

✦ If none of that works then you might also want look into Emotional Freedom Techniques (www.emofree.com). This might sound a bit new-age – EFT is a needle-free version of acupuncture that claims to provide relief from pain, disease and emotional issues – and I wouldn't mention it at all if it weren't for studies showing that, to date, EFT has had a 100 per cent success rate with yippers.

✦ Finally, read Hank Haney's *Fix the Yips Forever*.

Crazy though it might seem, big bucks and big brains are coming together in the search for a yips cure. However, there are a number of relatively simple cures before you resort to this.

THE THRILL OF MATCHPLAY

In the genteel game of golf, it doesn't hurt to throw down the gauntlet of head-to-head competition every once in a while; bring it on...

Matchplay is golf at its sportiest, as much a battle of wits as ability. If you've got a grudge against someone, it's far more satisfying to beat them 6&5 than by six shots in a medal round.

MATCHPLAY MOVES

There's so much psychology tied up in matchplay that it's worth running through a few tips that might give you the mental edge. This isn't gamesmanship, just cunning tactics.

The Ryder Cup is matchplay at its pulsating best, and always fantastic entertainment. I'm so hooked on the game that I get excited about the Madeira Island Open, so you can imagine what the Ryder Cup does for me.

✦ Don't start out trying to match your opponent shot for shot. Play the course. If it's really tight coming down the stretch you might then take more notice of what your opponent is doing.

✦ If it's close, hit your tee shot shorter than your opponent's and stiff your approach shot first, thus putting all the pressure on them.

✦ Concede a few two/three-footers early on, but make your foe putt out on the later holes. That will deprive your rival of any confidence-building short putts early on, and also introduce an element of doubt as to why you made him or her hole this one but gave the others.

✦ Always expect your opponent to play a brilliant shot or hole a long putt so you won't be upset when it happens. If it lips out, count it as a bonus.

✦ Always speak positively about yourself and believe what you say.

✦ Never give up when you're down, and never go easy when you're up.

Foolish Words

I remember a school match in which I went four down after four. As my opponent and I walked to the 5th tee, we started talking. He mentioned he was useless at matchplay and that, before today, had never won a single game.

I'm no Jack Nicklaus when it comes to tactics, but I didn't need to be to take advantage of his pessimism and distrust of his own game. Not surprisingly, he crumbled when I started playing a bit better and I beat him 3&2.

PLAYING IN THE WIND

You've played a sheltered inland course all your life but you're off to Scotland for some links golf. The first course you play is Royal Dornoch, and while the view from the 1st tee is pretty special, the gale blowing in off the North Sea could be a problem.

The wind at a coastal course seems very different to that which you might face in the sheltered suburbs. For a start it smells of salt, but more than that, it's cold and probably strong enough to render your yardage planner all but meaningless.

For the first-time visitor to a links, the wind can be totally overwhelming. You can fight it all day and always, always come off second best. Downwind your ball flies much lower than expected, pitches well short of the green and still seems to be picking up speed as it vanishes over the back. Into the wind you'll lose your hat and, just as bad, your ball will balloon into the air before dropping to the ground halfway to the hole.

To put it simply, you've got to expect higher scores in strong winds. It's inevitable. However, there are a few measures you can take to limit the damage, and even make the wind work for you.

HEAD ON
If you're on the tee using a driver, tee the ball a little lower, move it back an inch in your stance, grip the club a little lighter and focus on making a smooth swing. Solid contact is much more important than swing speed. Try to hit the ball hard and you'll most likely impart too much backspin and the ball will rise and fall like a paper plane. Just aim to 'sweep' through the ball, rather than 'hit' it.

You can apply a similar method to your iron approach shots. Take more club, grip down the handle a little, play the ball back in your stance and make an easy swing. Abbreviate your follow-through and above all don't impart too much backspin by hitting the ball hard. That just sends the ball too high and it lands well short of the green.

When hitting into the wind I picture Ernie Els' smooth rhythm. Although his clubhead is moving very fast, the acceleration in his swing seems very gentle and unhurried.

DOWNWIND
Playing downwind is a bittersweet combination of longer drives coupled with impossible-to-stop approach shots. Tee the ball higher with the driver, position it half an inch forward in your stance, get the feeling you're swinging up on the ball and launch it high into the sky where it can catch a free ride.

When approaching the green, just make your best judgement of where to land the ball. It could be on the front edge of the green or 50 yards short. If you can't land it short because there's a stream or bunker in front of the green, the best you can realistically expect is to go to the back of the green or over it. But that's not so bad. It's better than getting wet or chopping about in a pot bunker.

Walking back down a steep mountain can almost feel as tough as climbing up. Similarly, playing downwind can often be as tricky as hitting into it.

CROSSWINDS

There are two schools of thought for playing in a crosswind. The first is to counter a left-to-right wind by hitting a draw, and a right-to-left wind with a fade; meaning that the ball should fly fairly straight and stop quickly. The second is to play a normal shot, simply allowing the wind to push the ball in the direction it's moving.

I'd say the second option is probably the safer of the two for most amateurs, but bear in mind if you do go 'with' the wind your ball will effectively be travelling downwind towards the end of its flight, so won't stop quickly.

PUTTING

In a strong wind, putting becomes extremely tricky as not only does the wind

Long Way Out, Easy Home

On a chilly November day a few years back, my mate Dave and I took on the Old Course at St Andrews in a howling gale. We considered spending the day in the local inn, but I'm very glad we didn't.

Those familiar with the 1st hole know it's not much more than a drive and pitching wedge in normal conditions, but on this day I hit a career drive followed by a career 4-iron and made it over the burn in front of the green with just about a foot to spare. To reach the par-5 5th, I needed a driver, two 3-woods and a 6-iron while I went over the back of the 530-yard 14th with a driver and a 5-iron.

My score wasn't fit for this or any other publication, but I don't remember too many rounds as enjoyable as this one.

affect the ball it also makes it difficult to keep your body and head still. So first of all, for better balance just widen your stance slightly. Also, hover the putter just above the ground when you address the ball, because if you ground the club and the ball moves or oscillates in the wind you are deemed to have moved it and must add a penalty stroke.

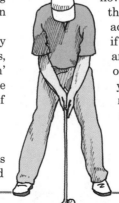

With a wide base, the wind can't blow you over.

GETTING A GRIP

If the grip of a club is worn and shiny, you'll hold the club tighter to prevent it from slipping. A tight grip leads to tight forearms, tight forearms lead to a poor release of the clubhead, and a poor release usually ends up short and in the trees.

Some pros change their grips every week which strikes me as a touch overzealous, but I suppose if my livelihood depended partly on my equipment I'd want to keep it in tip-top condition as well. Weekend golfers should re-grip their clubs at least once a year and wash them with warm, soapy water once a month. With a clean, tacky grip your hold on the club will soften automatically, and you'll release the clubhead powerfully once again.

Many take their clubs to the pro-shop to be re-gripped. But it's not exactly rocket science, and you can find all the necessary bits and pieces online, so if you want to save a few bob, do it yourself. You'll need:

+ A utility knife. Use a hook blade on graphite shafts to avoid damage.
+ Grip solvent. White spirit works well, but odourless, non-toxic, non-flammable products are preferable.
+ Two-sided ¾-in (2-cm)-wide grip tape.
+ A vice and a rubber vice clamp.

PROCEDURE

First, choose the grip. Make sure the butt end is the correct diameter and that it's the right thickness for your hands – if you have large hands and/or consistently hook the ball, try a thicker grip. Slicers and those with small hands should try a thinner grip.

Place the club in the vice, using the rubber vice clamp. Starting at the thin end, cut along the length of the grip, peel it off and scrape away the old tape.

Spiral wrap the tape around the shaft making sure not to go down further than the end of the new grip, and extending the tape about a half inch past the butt end. Peel the back off, and twist the end of the tape inserting it into the end of the shaft to prevent solvent getting in.

Cover the grip's vent hole with your finger (or plug it with a tee) and pour solvent into the grip. Then pour the solvent from the grip over the tape, and quickly slide the new grip on to the shaft.

Make sure the grip is aligned correctly. Give it a twist if necessary.

Finally, leave it to dry overnight.

TEXAS SCRAMBLE

There are more ways to score at golf than there are pages in this book, and I couldn't possibly tell you what they all were even if I had the space. However, the Texas scramble is a personal favourite, and you should give it a try.

Since I moved to America, my favourite format has been the extremely popular four-player scramble, ideally Texan, in which a certain number of drives from each member of the team must be used – a restriction that adds an element of strategy and means that nobody goes home feeling a complete loser because none of their drives were used.

Many readers will be familiar with the scramble, but for those who aren't I suggest you enter one as soon as possible, as this particular format involves just the right mix of feisty competition and team bonding. You and your teammates will celebrate your birdies and curse your missed putts in unison, and any time four men or women celebrate or commiserate together a real bond can be formed.

One of the many beauties of the scramble is that you can take four otherwise hopeless golfers and turn them into a 65-shooting dream team by combining their rare solid drive, occasional sound approach and sporadic good putting with the huge dollop of luck needed for each of the players to stagger their flashes of good play effectively. Thus you get teams in which only one, maybe two, members are playing well and end up with 60 or, by failing to take advantage of good approach play, you can have teams with 15 birdie putts and three eagle putts, but who end up only four under par, which is what happened to a team I was part of last year. To say that was frustrating doesn't quite capture it.

Among my other favourite games are Stableford, Shamble, String, Skins and Switch which, you'll probably notice, all start with an 'S'. I don't think that's a pre-requisite for a good game, but you never know.

The great thing about Texas scramble is that you stand or fall as a team. Mind you, if someone misses a six-footer to win, you can blame it all on them.

WHERE TO BUY YOUR KIT

I've bought from on-course pro-shops, high-street golf superstores, online retailers, online auctions and even a 'for sale' ad in the local newspaper. Not surprisingly, I've had varied results.

The general rule is never to buy so much as a tee without trying it first. Well that's not quite true; feel free to buy a tee, just never ever buy clubs without hitting them first, ideally on a golf course where you can see the flight of the ball. A driving range is okay, but bear in mind you'll probably be hitting off mats that give a slightly unrealistic feel at impact. Nets are no good for testing as you have no idea where the ball might have ended up.

Like racquets, rods and cues, every golf club is unique. Two may look exactly alike, have come out of the same factory, be the same length, loft and lie, and have grips the same thickness, but somehow they just feel different. While one might not sit quite right with you, another might just have that 'feel' about it. In short, you need to hit both to find the one you like.

If the pro lets you out on the course to test new equipment, offers helpful, friendly advice and matches or is close to the price on the high street, I see no reason to go anywhere else.

IN THE PRO-SHOP
In a perfect world I'd buy all my equipment from the pro-shop. I could test everything on the adjoining course prior to making any decisions and honour the hard-working pro who's struggling to compete with the superstores. The prices on the high street or online are simply too good to ignore a lot of the time, but to combat this, many pros band together to form buying groups that can often meet the superstores' prices. Find one of these and your search may be over. The combination of low price, knowledgeable service and being able to test is invaluable.

THE HIGH-STREET SHOP
They offer a superb variety and invariably great prices, but often the only place a high-street store will let you test the club is in their nets. If budget is your only consideration and you don't mind the possibility of souring your relationship, you could ask your club pro if you can test a club at the course then go and buy it somewhere cheaper; but don't expect the same kind of friendly service next time you pop in.

ON THE WEB
Again, the internet offers great prices and choice, but you can't test the kit before you shell out what could be some serious cash. Most retailers offer a money-back guarantee, of course, but returning clubs can be tedious in the extreme.

ONLINE AUCTIONS
The price is usually right if you're familiar with online auction sites such

as eBay. But what happens when the club arrives and the picture you saw on the website turns out to have been somewhat misleading? You may have a money-back guarantee, but you'll probably have seven days to notify the seller; while some don't specify a return policy at all. Although I had many reservations, I did buy a driver in an online auction once. Luckily, it fitted me well, but it took a lot of patience to find it, and a very late night to win it.

There are thousands of sites selling golf kit on the internet. If you know what you're looking for, are confident an online fitting is adequate (or have the specs from a more thorough fitting to hand) you can find what you need at a fantastic price. You just have to keep your fingers crossed that what arrives on your doorstep is what you think you ordered.

THE LOCAL PAPER

This is not the most sophisticated way to find clubs, but if it's a rusty set of second-hand clubs with the 5-iron missing that you're looking for then it can't hurt to have a look. Actually, I bought some clubs from a guy advertising in the paper once. They were horrible clubs in terrible condition, but I didn't know them from a set of brand-new Forged Callaway X-Tour Irons at the time. So what did I care?

GOLFING MATTERS

Walk if You Can

You have to take these stats with a very large pinch of salt because everybody's metabolism is different and every course is different, but even when riding a buggy, the average golfer will burn an average of 300 calories an hour. Carry your clubs and walk and you'll burn up to twice that amount.

Golf gets a bad rap for its limited athletic demands, but apparently one hour of walking a golf course has the same effect as an hour of ballroom dancing. That seems incredible to me, but I've got the figures right here in front of me. My reliable source also informs me that I could use up exactly the same number of calories playing golf as I would scrubbing the kitchen floor on my hands and knees for an hour. I know which I'd rather.

Whatever anyone says, carrying your bag and walking the length of a golf course with its numerous ups and downs is very good exercise. Sure, it's not running a four-and-a-half-minute mile, playing football or cycling up a mountain. But it certainly beats sitting on your butt watching television.

🏌 THE WET STUFF

Whether it's a tempestuous ocean or tranquil mill pond, the sight of water can wreak havoc with a golfer's sensibilities. We see getting wet as so final, so absolute, so irrevocable. And Bobby Jones didn't help matters when he said the difference between finding a bunker and a water hazard was like the difference between a car crash and a plane crash.

Sure, you may think there's no way back from the watery depths; but this is dangerous territory. After all, if you find the water on a par 3, play another ball from the drop zone, then hole the putt you can walk off with a bogey four – the same as if you'd hit a nice shot to the green but three-putted. Likewise, on a par 4 you can find a stream short of the green, drop, pitch and putt for a five, or even on a par 5, you can walk off with a par if you pitch and putt after dropping.

Of course, I would never recommend finding the water, but doing so needn't carry with it such an air of finality. As we've seen above, the penalty for finding a lake, stream, pond or sea can often be no worse than three-putting or chunking a chip. And you're actually better off than the poor chump who sailed over the water and the green and flew out of bounds. He doesn't have a drop zone up near the green to help him. He's got to go all the way back to where he played the original shot and face that daunting carry over the water again.

I think part of the reason we get so intimidated by water, besides the unhelpful notion that we will automatically lose the hole or make a double-bogey should we find it, is that the feeling of making it over to dry ground is so uplifting that should we fail it might ruin our day. Fine, I might be clutching at straws, but I know that's sometimes how I feel when I arrive on the 6th tee at my local course. I know that if I fly the water and land on the green my tea will taste that bit better, regardless of what I do the rest of the round. The solution, I suppose, is to somehow blot the water out.

Just imagine the pounding surf and crashing waves aren't there. It's merely another flat, dull par 3 – no big deal at all.

TAKE IT TO THE COURSE

No doubt you're familiar with the routine. As you hammer range balls far into the distance, you have total command of your swing. Every ball bows dutifully to your whim. The trick is to take that form onto the course.

A five-yard draw, you ask? No problem. A high, looping fade? Exactly how high and loopy would you like that? Between the legs, ricochet off your golf bag, five-yard draw and a high looping fade before dropping like a stone next to the hole? Well, perhaps not, but nevertheless you still feel good on the range.

As you move to the 1st tee, however, the good feelings drain away and the silky, powerful move you had going ten minutes before has turned into a lurch. You slice your opening drive onto a parallel fairway and it continues like this for six holes at the end of which you're ready to rip up your scorecard. Of course, from the 7th to the 18th you play like a dream.

What happened to the on-demand fades and 300-yard drives? It's a mental thing, obviously. Not overly concerned with results on the range – you know that a bad shot won't affect your score – you grip the club lightly, ease the club away smoothly and hit through the ball like Ernie Els. On the course, however, your thinking changes entirely. Apathy turns to anxiety because your shots have now become extremely important.

It does you no good to jump so quickly from calm indifference to acute nervous tension. You need to adopt similar habits

If the 1st tee shot looks anything like that at Machrihanish in Scotland, it will help if you know what to expect and have imagined the shot before you arrive. Otherwise you are going to get one heck of a shock.

on both the range and course to make the move from one to the other less significant. The pre-shot routine is so important that you should use it for every shot you hit, wherever you are. It may also help to mix up the shots that you hit on the range when warming up. Don't hit a lot in succession with the same club. Always aim at something. And try to picture what you'll be facing on the course, especially your 1st tee shot. Now, when you get to the 1st tee, it probably won't seem so scary and you'll hopefully hit the ground running.

T-SQUARES AND WEIGHTED CLUBS

Sometimes pounding balls on the range just isn't enough. You have to introduce something different to stimulate your practice session. Drills are great and a training aid can help too. Just don't go spending all your money on useless gadgets and gizmos.

Time was when a white plastic ball with holes in it was all the practice aid one needed. You'd take it out to the back garden and swing away freely knowing you couldn't hit it hard enough to clear the back fence let alone smash any windows. They were safe, cheap and who knows, might even have helped you with your golf.

The ludicrous number of training aids that are now available serves to illustrate just how bad at golf we all are. After all, if we were any good, we wouldn't be buying these things and encouraging more would-be inventors to introduce their latest, greatest contraptions to help us with a part of our game we didn't know needed help.

By purchasing dozens of training aids, you are, in a way, convincing yourself that you are rubbish. That may or may not be true, but I'm not convinced a closet full of swing vests, swing balls, swing setters, speed sticks and hinged clubs is the answer to your problems. I'm not saying that buying a training aid isn't a good idea – far from it, there are many fine products out there. But overloading on the stuff just reminds you what a desperately difficult game it is we play, and remembering how difficult golf can be is not going to help you master it any quicker.

My suggestion is to limit yourself to one, maybe two, training aids, namely a weighted club and a T-square. (The 'Crotch Hook' which attaches to your head and genitals and pulls sharply on the latter should you raise your head too early might also be an option for golfers who look up before impact.) The weighted club not only develops the muscles you

Danger: Golf

My dad used to own a training aid that clearly wasn't meant for a dumb kid like his own. It consisted of a golf ball attached to a length of elastic attached to a long spike that you stuck in the ground. When you hit the ball, it flew round in a circle and, the idea was, landed right back at your feet.

One day, I absent-mindedly pulled on the ball and the spike came flying out of the ground. Fortunately my face was concealed behind my arm, through which the spike travelled. It all happened so quickly that it was perhaps five or six seconds before I realized the spike had entered one side of my arm and come out the other. I ran into the kitchen and calmly asked my father if I was going to die. He said probably not, but that we should go to hospital just in case. I survived to tell the tale, but I hope the 'Elasticized Golf Training Aid with Spike' didn't.

use to power your golf swing, it also helps you generate greater width and tempo; while the T-square ensures better alignment and ball position. Really, what more do you need?

Not only do you look a bit silly, you may not be helping your scores as much as you think.

The Irritating Golfer

Although I'd sooner be washed up on a desert island with a golfer than anyone else, there are factions of our subculture that do not toe the line, as it were – golfers who exhibit irksome, disrespectful and just downright annoying habits.

I wouldn't say I'm overly picky or judgemental, in fact I hope I'm good company. But if you do any of the following, then I can see we're going to have a problem.

+ Cheat.
+ Repeatedly make or receive non-emergency calls on your phone.
+ Step all over my putting line.
+ Talk loudly.
+ Keep giving yourself four-foot putts.
+ Pace off the yardage to the hole and throw bits of grass in the air despite the fact you're 22 over par.
+ Fail to replace your divots, rake the bunkers you play out of or repair pitch marks.
+ Give me a running commentary of your round.
+ Tell me what I'm doing wrong and give me swing advice when I didn't ask for it.
+ Curse strongly your bad luck and yourself for bad shots.
+ Or in any other way be perceived as taking our little game way too seriously.

BOOKS

There are over 25,000 golf books in the USGA library alone. I hope you'll forgive me if I don't mention all of them here, but there is space to list a few that are definitely worth the read.

The Golf library at home is coming on nicely.

The avid golf reader's library probably averages a dozen instruction books, far more than anyone needs or for that matter gets round to reading. Common to most collections are *Five Lessons: The Modern Fundamentals of Golf* by Ben Hogan, and Harvey Penick's *Little Red Golf Book*. I own both and have, at different stages of life, benefited greatly from both – *Five Lessons* when I was young and open to complex theory, *Little Red Golf Book* more recently when I needed small chunks of wisdom that didn't require me to sit down and think too hard.

Among other classic instruction books are Jack Nicklaus' *My Golden Lessons*, Ernest Jones's *Swing the Clubhead* (see pages 26–7), Percy Boomer's *On Learning Golf* and Tommy Armour's *How to Play Your Best Golf All the Time*. For putting, you can't really beat Dave Pelz's *Putting Bible* unless, of course, you think a book this thick is slightly over the top for the art of hitting a ball into a hole with a stick.

Those in need of help with the psychological side of the game should read Bob Rotella's *Golf Is Not a Game of Perfect*, or Gio Valiante's *Fearless Golf: Conquering the Mental Game*. I read Rotella's book recently and it certainly helped unclog a few synapses.

Every golfer's coffee table needs a huge, doorstop picture book weighing it down. Several worthy of the most discerning coffee tables have been published lately, the most notable Jim Finegan's enormous *Where Golf is Great*. Another beauty is *Golf Courses: Fairways of the World*, which features photographer Dave Cannon's superb images.

MY ALL-TIMERS
My favourites among the hundreds of golf books in my house are neither instructional nor collections of great photographs, however. *The Greatest Game Ever Played*, *The Grand Slam* and *The Match* all by Mark Frost are superbly researched and real page-turners. But my absolute number one is a collection of 31 silly short stories featuring characters such as Rollo Podmarsh, Cuthbert Banks and the 'Oldest Member'. First published in 1973 and subsequently reprinted 19 times, PG Wodehouse's *The Golf Omnibus*, is as enjoyable now as it was the day I bought it 18 years ago. I've only read it once this year though, so I might just dust it off this evening.

⚘ ON TEES

Before William Bloxsom and Arthur Douglas patented the first ever portable teeing device in 1889, golfers had to shape a small mound of sand in order to raise their ball off the ground. Bloxsom and Douglas's tee was a fairly crude design but it set the world of tees in motion.

Today there is a vast range of lengths and shapes to choose from 2⅛ in, 2⅜ in, 2¾ in and 3¼ in standard shape, 7mm, 12mm, 19mm, 25mm, 32mm, 40mm and 50mm Castle tees, thin shank/small head tees, Brush Tees, Rip Tips, Eco tees, Velocitees, KORECTEES, Ti-Tees, PerfectTees, E-Tees featuring an internal spring, A-Balance Tees, Stinger Tees, CertainTees, Bazooka Hybrid Tees and so on. There's even a tool called the T-Rite that uses the 'latest breakthrough in consistent tee height setting technology' to ensure you tee your ball at the correct height every time (one imagines a mob of mad scientists working furiously in a secret laboratory in the Nevada desert to take tee-height setting technology to the next level).

The tee pocket in my bag is full of white, wooden, 3¼ in jumbo tees. You need these extra-long ones in order to tee the ball high enough for your mega-headed titanium driver. Some players, most notably Sergio Garcia, tee the ball very low – the top of the driver is higher than the top of the ball. The shape and speed of his swing is very different to most amateurs', however, so do yourself a favour and perch your ball up nice and high.

There are, of course, shorter tees available that are designed for use with an iron, say on a par 3, but you know what I do? I just push my 3¼ in jumbo tee further into the ground.

One wonders about a world with quite so many different types of tee to choose from.

DIFFERENT HEIGHTS FOR DIFFERENT SHOTS

For all the complexities of the golf swing and the various parts that can go wrong, the accuracy of your shots could well be affected by nothing more complex than the height at which you tee the ball.

If you hook the ball with your driver, try teeing it a little lower. This encourages a slightly steeper attack from outside the target line which results in a high slice. If you slice – and who doesn't? – try teeing it higher. This promotes a shallower path from inside the target line and consequently a sweet little draw.

To encourage a fade, tee it low; for a draw, tee it high.

DOING IT AT HOME

There are loads of devices, both electronic and mechanical, available to help you practise at home. Most of them are expensive and probably unnecessary. Cheapskate that I am, I prefer to use stuff I already have, like mirrors, walls and chairs.

You may not actually hit any balls, but there's a lot you can do in the comfort of your own home, with the television on in the corner and a pot of tea brewing, to improve your golf.

Mirrors

Facing a mirror, you can check:

+ Your grip.
+ Ball position.
+ The length of your backswing.
+ Extent of your hip and shoulder turn.
+ How your head moves.

Then side-on you can make sure:

+ That your shoulders, knees and feet all line up.
+ Your posture is sound.
+ You don't bring the club back too far on the inside (a common problem with slicers).
+ Your swingplane is good (the angle of the shaft halfway back is the same as the shaft angle at address).
+ Your hands are nice and high at the top of your backswing.
+ The clubface is square (45° to the ground) or close to square at the top of the backswing.
+ Your right knee remains flexed as you take the club up.

If you're going to separate your swing into sections, the place to do it is in front of a mirror. Make sure you're

getting the club into the desired positions and swing the club in slow motion to reinforce the feeling you want to replicate on the course.

Don't just style your hair in the mirror. Put it to better use by checking your grip and posture.

Walls

A wall (I'm assuming you have these in your house) is excellent for helping you with swingpath. Stand facing a wall a few feet away and take your club to the top. Come down slowly making sure the clubhead gets no closer to the wall than it was at address. Do that slowly a hundred times and the over-the-top move which produces pull-slices will slowly disappear. Another way to establish a downswing that attacks the ball from the inside is to address a ball (an imaginary one is just fine) with your back to the wall. Take your club slowly to the top until the clubhead rests against it. Pull the club down slowly until your hands are about hip-high with the clubhead still touching the wall. By now, slicers will have thrown the clubhead out in front of them, but you're approaching the ball from the inside and in good position to hit a gentle draw.

CHIPPING

Chipping balls into an easy chair, an upturned umbrella, sand box, under or over a swing or lobbing them over the fence (which only works if your next-door neighbour is understanding) is a great way to improve your feel for shots around the green.

PUTTING

Putting into a glass or your kids' plastic golf holes always works, unless your carpets have some heavy decorative weave that throws your ball off line. There are even ingenious devices such as the 'Puttacup' that allow you to putt into an actual hole.

Get a feel for the speed of Augusta National's greens by putting on hardwood floors.

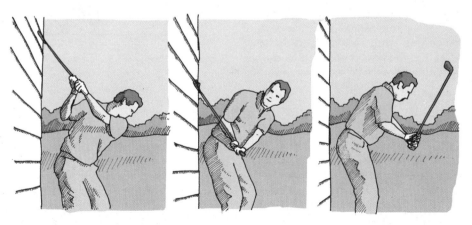

By repeating this drill over and over you will learn what the correct downswing path feels like and eliminate the over-the-top swingpath (on the right).

THE UNHELPFUL LESSON

I'm sure we're all inherently good people, so when we see a friend hacking their way to another triple bogey we instinctively feel a desire to offer some assistance. The trouble is we often don't wait to be asked.

But here's the problem, or rather problems. Years spent playing golf badly don't really qualify amateurs to teach the game, and the 'lesson' they have to offer is probably based on some swing analysis they saw on the television or read in a magazine, meaning it's factually correct but perhaps not relevant to the person they're teaching. They also tend to forget their 'pupil' is not a professional athlete, doesn't practise every day, and doesn't own custom-built clubs; rather they are a stiff, slightly overweight, once-a-weeker who hasn't had a lesson in years and with a collection of clubs based on low price rather than high performance.

BACKWARD IN COMING FORWARD
I'd suggest biting your tongue unless your buddy asks for help. Most problems are best addressed on the range after the round, not while it is still in progress.

Out on the course just concentrate on getting your stricken partner back to the clubhouse without him or her upending their bag of clubs into the

lake (which is in any case where most of their balls now reside). However, if there is a useful piece of advice then try to choose an appropriate time to remind your playing partner of the importance of tempo. It's most likely that as their grip has tightened the rhythm has all but disappeared and their all-round game has disintegrated.

Keeping your head down is common sense, right? Actually, making a conscious effort to do so might be bad for both your back and your shot.

COMMON SWING MYTHS
Of all the tips ever offered between well-meaning but misinformed friends, 'keep your head down' and 'keep your left arm straight' are unquestionably the most common. These old chestnuts have been doing the rounds for decades and while both sound perfectly reasonable they can be extremely toxic.

'No mate, you're doing it all wrong. You've got to do it more like me.'

GOING OFF PISTE

I've done some dumb things in my time, but none dumber than this. I was in the eastern Washington town of Spokane for a short break with my wife when I turned on the radio and listened to a guy talk about a tournament taking place on a ski hill just to the north. It all went wrong from there.

The man on the radio said that if listeners could get there within a couple of hours they could still enter. It sounded promising and we had nothing planned, so I turned the car around.

Arriving at the 49 Degrees North Ski Resort, I learned that rather than playing a legitimate course over flattish junior slopes at the base of the 5,774ft mountain, we would in fact be taking a lift to the very top and playing up and down black runs with names like Last Chance, Tombstone and Crusher.

After an hour-long ride I jumped off, looked around for a golf hole and began wondering what in God's name I had gotten involved in. The 1st measured well over 1,000 yards and dropped almost 1,000 feet.

I watched as a school teacher in the group ahead of mine hit a tee shot with a 3-wood that hung in the air for 25 seconds or more, before eventually landing just a few yards to the right of the target – a white painted circle some 20ft in diameter. A golfer for only a short time, he was pleased to learn his 1,000-yard 3-wood was roughly three or four times longer than any 3-wood Tiger Woods had ever hit.

In stark contrast, my opening tee shot sliced way right into a dark and eerie forest in which I took numerous hacks only to emerge cut to ribbons by brambles and pointy branches. The rules did account for such misfortune, allowing players to place their ball within a club's

Ski hills were meant for one thing... and it wasn't golf. Sadly, the UX Open was last played in 2004. I say 'sadly', but somehow I don't miss it that much.

length of where they had found it. But a single club was never enough to find a half decent lie amongst the weeds, thistle and assorted shrubbery growing on the 'fairways'.

The 5th was without doubt the hardest 'golf hole' I've ever played – about 800 yards long up a near 45° incline with about 25 yards of space between the pines. It took me 45 minutes to make a 12.

Almost hyper-ventilating, I finished the ten holes in 68, 29 over par and in third-to-last place. My wife asked if it had been fun. 'No,' I said.

THE GOLF TRIP

In 1963, Eddie Pola and George Wyle composed 'It's the Most Wonderful Time of the Year', a jolly jingle about Christmas. I suspect Messrs Pola and Wyle weren't golfers. Sure, Christmas is great, but nothing beats the golf trip with your mates.

I think a good golf trip should be taken once a year and become a tradition, something you get excited about months before you leave. And it should be recorded electronically or in a scrapbook, anywhere but your failing memory. That way you'll never forget Bob's hole-in-one at La Manga six years ago, or the time Bill fell flat on his face on the 1st tee at Ballybunion following a particularly heavy evening at McMunn's on Main Street.

WHO'S GOING?

For it to become something really special, the same people should be involved each year, though you should expect some change in personnel as diminishing finances, failing health, and growing family ties will all inevitably take their toll as the years go by.

The ideal number for a trip is four, or multiples of four, so you can play together every day. If there are five, seven or nine, you'll have to split up which makes scoring and bonding that bit more difficult. You know who the ideal four are, and it doesn't bode well if you have a hard time deciding who should go.

WHERE TO GO?

The world is your oyster nowadays, but it obviously depends where you are starting from and how far your budget will stretch. The UK and Ireland always have plenty to offer. In Europe, Spain and Portugal are old favourites, but Turkey is coming on strong, while France, Italy or the Czech Republic offer something a bit different.

Dubai is also seriously gearing up for golf tourists, South Africa is definitely worth the flight, especially if you like wine, and playing in Australia is a must at least once in your life. New Zealand possesses some of the world's most beautiful courses and is worthy of a trip

For a few days every year, you're as free as a bird – just you and your buddies playing golf. Good times.

in its own right, but can also be combined with a trip Down Under.

Thailand, Malaysia, Vietnam and China are probably best for the party that has played everywhere else, although the region's swelling number of golf resorts is making this once improbable trip ever more enticing.

Then there's America. Home to roughly two-thirds of the world's courses, the US is easy to get to, relatively inexpensive, has a superb infrastructure and a wealth of accommodation options. The courses are invariably well maintained and, as long as you go to Arizona, South Carolina, Florida or California, the weather is good year round.

If you're going by plane, you need to decide if you're taking your clubs with you, sending them to your destination with a luggage-handling company, or hiring clubs when you arrive. Personally, I think the trip is expensive enough without shipping or hiring clubs, so I take mine with me in a heavy-duty golf club travel bag.

If you can only spare a weekend there are plenty of websites offering packages. Just try to make it at least a two-night stay so you can really get out of your everyday routine.

ITINERARY

On a five-day trip, I'd say you should be playing golf on at least three of them, if not four. You can play 36 holes all five days, of course, just don't include me. After three or four straight days of golf I prefer to do something different

and come back to the course on day five raring to go again. Alternatively, plan 18 holes for early mornings and have 'free time' in the afternoons. As for eating, it makes for a more memorable trip if you can all eat together in the evenings, provided you're all still getting on with each other.

PACKAGE OR INDEPENDENT?

It makes sense to have all your tee-times and accommodation pre-booked and, if you can afford it, a vehicle and driver to ferry you about. If you're driving yourself, hire as big a car as you can afford (big enough for four players, four golf bags and four sets of luggage) and take it in turns to drive.

I have been on a trip where the only thing that was pre-booked was the flight (we didn't even know which courses we were going to play) and while it was great fun, I wouldn't choose that approach again. It's far less hassle to book and pay for everything (apart from drinks, tips, new golf balls and gifts for the family) in advance.

FORMAT

You really should have a tournament in which individuals accumulate points as the trip progresses. Vary the format each day – Stableford, foursome, better-ball, individual gross, two-man shambles, and so on – and add in all sorts of side shows like birdies, fairways hit, greens in regulation and number of putts. Have fun creating your own scoring system and award prizes at the end of the trip.

HANDICAPS

It is perfectly possible to enjoy a lifetime's golf without ever owning an official handicap. However, although that is certainly true, it doesn't quite paint the whole picture, as it isn't possible to experience everything the game has to offer without one.

I'll be perfectly honest and say that, currently, I do not own a handicap. Why? Several reasons really, most of them centring around a woeful lack of time for 'hobbies' and a lack of ready cash. These days, you actually don't need piles of money to get a handicap as you don't necessarily have to join a private golf club. You can just sign up with any of the commercial entities that offer a handicapping service (more of that later). But though I'll forever love the game and play whenever gaps in between work and family commitments allow it, I must admit I do not place as much importance on acquiring, keeping and improving a handicap as I used to. I know it's merely one of life's many phases, however, and that when the kids have flown the nest, I'll be back on the course every day sweating over every 0.1 of a stroke.

REASONS TO GET A HANDICAP
With a handicap you can:
+ Play at most courses around the world. Anyone can play at municipal and pay-and-play courses, but if you want to tee it up at a private club you'll invariably need some proof of your ability, and that means a handicap certificate.
+ To measure your performance more consistently over time.
+ Accurate, official handicaps help prevent you coming up against bandits – golfers who say they're off 18 when, in actual fact, they're nearer a 10.

HOW TO GET A HANDICAP
Join a private club that is affiliated with a handicapping body (such as CONGU in the UK). It's unlikely any private club is going to have you, however, unless you already have a handicap.

Handicap Bandits

A bandit (sandbagger in the US) is the untrustworthy bounder who intentionally doctors or lies about his true handicap in an effort to win valuable prizes and bets. When the stakes are low he will purposefully play badly, or he will not enter his better rounds into handicap maintenance software and thus artificially inflate his handicap. When the big money game or tournament with the big first prize rolls around he now has a few 'extra' strokes to play with. At worst, the bandit is a cad, a cheat and a two-bit hustler; at best... a cad, a cheat and a two-bit hustler.

There's a difference, of course, between someone who has an unexpected good day and beats their handicap handily and a committed, calculating bandit. Members of the first group are to be congratulated. Members of the second must be identified and run out of town.

This used to create a bit of a chicken or egg-type conundrum – you couldn't get a handicap unless you were a member of a golf club, but you couldn't join a golf club unless you had a handicap. Now, however, beginners and transient golfers can pay annual dues to one of several handicap certificate suppliers.

You'll need one of these to prove to the club that although you're only passing through, you're no hacker. It's a good idea to contact the club in advance though to make sure your handicap certificate will be accepted.

MAINTAINING A HANDICAP

If you think I'm going to waste valuable space by explaining how your handicap is set and can then increase or decrease under the system, then I'm afraid you are very much mistaken. I couldn't possibly summarize it in a few short lines, so just let me point you in the direction of www.congu.com and www.handicapmaster.org, which will tell you all you need to know.

THE ART OF GIVING

My drawers are full of golf gifts. I'm grateful for the thought, of course, but really my heart sinks as I unwrap yet another trinket.

I've seen golf-themed light switch plates, coasters, key racks, mugs, cufflinks, shower curtains, postboxes, towels, dressing gowns, lamp stands, doormats, salt and pepper shakers, teapots, plant pots, flasks, picture frames, fireplace sets, cutlery, watches, soap dispensers and house number plaques belonging to golfers who just don't have the heart to tell the giver that they really don't want this stuff and the money would actually be much better spent on a pair of socks.

If you can't summon up the courage to tell them yourselves, then just leave this book open on this page for them to find. Now, for all non-golfers reading this, do the golfer in your life a favour and get him or her a sleeve of balls instead. They're much easier to lose than some of the garbage you've given them over the years.

The motif gifts that actually do something like hold pens or mail are one thing. The furry frog with red and white cap and putter ornament is quite another, however, and should be outlawed.

CARRYING THE BAGS

Every now and again it's nice to have a caddie take you round. Besides performing the usual caddie duties, he or she could save you a few shots with some timely advice.

The last time I hired a caddie was at Pacific Dunes in Oregon two years ago. Rod was a strong young lad who not only carried my bag but also that of my partner.

At the 1st, 2nd and 3rd he was encouraging despite a barrage of bogeys. When dense fog rolled in at the 4th, he steered us well to the left of a precipitous clifftop off which we could very easily have fallen had we been by ourselves. At the 6th, he understandingly looked the other way when I found an impossibly deep bunker and failed to get out not once, not twice, but three times.

Having a caddie makes you feel like a professional, until you top your drive into a ditch that is.

Somewhere on the back nine he told us the story of a gentleman he had caddied for who shot 188. 'At least, that's what he said it was,' said Rod. 'I reckon it was nearer 250.' Then he told us about carrying for PGA Tour player Kirk Triplett, who had visited the course a few weeks previously. In terrible weather, Triplett shot 88 the first day, but improved to 64 the next.

I could go on but you get the picture. Rod was friendly, supportive, consoling, a well of information, full of good stories, and ever optimistic that my game might pick up at any moment. By the end of the round, we'd had such a good time, my mate and I had no problem bumping his fee up a little by way of thanks.

NOT ALL CADDIES ARE CREATED EQUAL

On another occasion, having somehow blagged a round at an extremely exclusive private club (its amazing what a well-worded letter can do), I ended up with an old geezer who arrived a few minutes late absolutely reeking of drink and who wasn't entirely sure where he had spent the night.

We didn't see eye to eye. I played poorly and he let me know it. He didn't actually tut or throw his hands in the air in disgust, but I could tell that he wanted to. A relic and an anachronism, he was a blast from the distant past, a far cry from today's usually polite and professional caddies.

YOU CADDIE HAS SEEN WORSE

The first time you hire a caddie it's likely you'll spend the first few holes worrying about the state of your golf and whether or not they've ever witnessed anyone play quite as badly. You'll want to perform as much for your caddie as yourself, and probably won't settle down until you've hit a few good shots or your caddie has told you that yes, he's caddied for dozens of golfers worse even than you.

CADDYING YOURSELF

If you're ever roped in to caddying for your dad, a friend or maybe Tiger Woods, you need to know the caddie's three most basic instructions; show up, keep up and shut up. Turn up well before the tee-time, don't lag behind and, as a general rule, don't speak unless spoken to. Of course, there are exceptions, and if it's your dad you are caddying for, feel free to tell him how ridiculous his no-pleat, drain-pipe trousers and fat white belt look on a man of his age.

GOLFING FOR COUPLES

Plenty of couples get along just fine on the course; however, unfortunately for my wife and I, we are not among their number.

About ten years ago my then fiancée, now wife, and I went for a quiet round, her first. Much to my pleasant surprise, by about the 3rd hole she was lofting the ball into the air as if she had been playing the game all her life. I began to envision the two of us forming a killer mixed foursome, hoisting all sorts of trophies and taking golf holidays together.

She seemed equally excited and, on the 5th, claimed golf was an easy game, and that if I were to give her lessons, well who knows...

It seemed like a reasonable idea at the time. I had been a teacher, after all, and it would be a wonderful opportunity to spend time together.

Our first lesson started smoothly enough, but after altering her posture she began shanking the ball. Quickly, things turned nasty. I became 'a total idiot who can't teach' while she was the 'nightmare pupil who thinks she knows it all but can't take instruction'.

The lessons stopped and for nine years she never once mentioned the game. Recently, however, she has started watching it on TV with me. I'd love for her to play again, and I still haven't ruled out those golfing holidays. But if she ever talks about lessons, I think I'll tell her about a teaching professional I know.

IT'S ALL IN YOUR MIND

We've seen how good course management can benefit your score without you having to lift a finger, and here's something else that could improve your golf with very little physical enterprise on your part. This game gets easier by the page.

Until fairly recently no one knew much about sports psychology and no one had any idea that thoughts moving in and out of their heads might help or hinder their performance. No one knew, for instance, that repeatedly cursing your own luck could poison your mind and prevent you from playing to the best of your ability. No one knew that telling yourself you were brilliant and that the last shot you played was truly a work of genius might actually help.

Now, of course, psychologists are as much a fixture on the driving range at tour events as swing gurus. Getting a little down on yourself? Quick, bring the mental coach in to perk you up. Need some inspiring words or a good mental image? The good doctor will see you now.

Pros are using anything they can within the rules to optimize their games and players not seeking the services of a sports psychologist are becoming

A psychologist is very much part of a tour player's entourage nowadays.

increasingly uncommon. But you're just a regular weekend player, so what's this got to do with you? What on earth do you need with a sports psychologist?

Alright, so maybe your unique style of play doesn't quite warrant the expense of a fully fledged sports shrink; but that doesn't mean you can't pinch a few of their tricks. After all you work on the physical side of your game, so why neglect the mental challenges?

The 'remain positive' mantra common to all sports psychologists' teachings will certainly help you. Okay, 'remain positive' might be a little vague, and in need of fleshing out – but it's a start.

Calmly tell yourself you can hit this shot, that you've done it before and can do it again. As psychologist Joe Kolezynski says, if you desire to change a negative belief into an empowering belief, you must rewire the negative neural track that already exists in the brain into a positive one by using self-talk and affirmations. What does that actually mean? Simple, you need to stop the self-condemnation, identify parts of your game that need improvement and create affirmations that you can say over and over to yourself. Make them short and specific. 'I am a putting machine and hole all 15ft putts,' is better than 'Yeah, I do okay. I hole my share of medium-range putts, but I suppose I could be a lot better. I'm pretty good at reading greens and aiming correctly, and if I could just get the speed right...' Kolezynski suggests the following process:

'I am Tiger Woods. I am Tiger Woods.'
Positive affirmations can certainly be good for
your game, but make them realistic and wait
until the house is empty before talking loudly to
yourself. You could scare the kids.

+ Sit upright in a comfortable chair.
+ Close your eyes and take a couple of minutes to relax.
+ Release your body's tight, sharp focus on the physical world by taking yourself to an even deeper level of relaxation.
+ Speak your affirmation aloud five times.
+ Do all this as often as possible.

Be patient with this. Don't expect results overnight – but keep at it and they'll arrive soon enough. In his book *The Art and Zen of Golf Learning* Michael Hebron takes it a step further, advising golfers to favour pictures and feelings over words of instruction. Picture how the club should move, he says, not the body.

RELAX, EASY, SMOOTH... OR NOT?

As well as telling them to keep their head down and their left arm straight, golfers are in the habit of urging their underperforming partners to relax, slow down and swing easy.

A lot of the time that's wise counsel, for who doesn't occasionally lose their rhythm? Sometimes, however, the words 'slow', 'relax' and 'easy' can be misinterpreted. Ernie Els might appear relaxed, even carefree, but rest assured, he is concentrating hard; and by the time most amateurs get their club to the top of the backswing, Els has already thundered through impact. He hits the ball incredibly hard, but his even tempo and supreme balance make his swing look easy.

Jack Nicklaus, among others, suggests that instead of swinging easy or relaxing, you should actually swing as hard as you can 'while still swinging rhythmically enough to keep the clubhead under control'.

There's a line between hard and reckless. When you catch the ball cleanly, pass the 280-yard mark and are still in perfect balance you'll know you're on the right side of it.

Swing like this and not only will you miss the fairway you'll do yourself a serious injury too.

THE HOME OF GOLF

The Old Course has been mentioned often enough in this book, and there's a fair chance you know all about it already. So let's find somewhere else to play and then, when we're done, head off into town to see what we can find.

At the time of writing (early 2008) the St Andrews Links Trust operates six golf courses. By the time you read this, there will be seven as the highly anticipated Castle Course, sandwiched between the east end of town and the privately owned St Andrews Bay golf courses, will be open. I've only seen pictures so can't really say too much about it other than if it plays as good as it looks then it's likely to run the Old Course a very close second in terms of popularity. That means the New Course will be demoted to third.

If you can't get a tee-time on the Old, don't worry the New is nearby. It costs half as much to play and is very nearly as good.

How a course as good as the New could possibly rank as low as third in a town of just 14,000 people is obviously a large part of what makes the place so special. The Jubilee is fantastic too, if a little difficult, and the charming Eden holds some very special memories as the first links course I ever played. The short Strathtyrum and par-3 Balgove courses

complete the Links Trust set, but the golf in the area certainly doesn't end there. Just east of town is Kingsbarns, another of the world's best links courses, while a bit further inland is the superb Dukes Course, and on Fife's south coast, just 20 minutes drive away, are Craighead, Balcomie, Elie, Leven and Lundin.

After the game, it's worth stopping by the Jigger Inn at the side of the Old Course's 17th green to watch a few stragglers trying to extricate themselves from the depths of the Road Hole Bunker. As night falls why not head to the Dunvegan for a bite to eat and a look at the photographs of famous golfers who have called in down the years.

Then head back to your digs, ideally Rusacks on Pilmour Links overlooking the Old Course's 18th hole or, if you're really in the money, the Old Course Hotel where, if it's July and you're in the Royal & Ancient Suite, you'd better have a very deep purse.

When you're done playing golf, check out the cathedral ruins and the grave of Young Tom Morris who won the Open four times between 1868 and 1872, but died at 24 on Christmas Day 1875, three months after the death of his wife and newborn baby.

CHANGES I'D LIKE TO SEE

It could be argued that golf is currently enjoying something of a golden age. The number one player in the world is the most recognizable figure in all of sport, while better equipment has made the game more fun for everyone. We shouldn't let it all go to our heads though.

In his absorbing book *The Future of Golf*, respected commentator Geoff Shackelford paints a bleak picture, saying the game is becoming too slow, too expensive and too boring. Five-hour rounds and ever-increasing green fees – inflated by 'signature' designs carrying the name of big-name players – are discouraging people from trying golf and forcing many existing golfers away, he says. The USGA and PGA Tours' insatiable appetites for cashing in on Tiger Woods' prominence is also sucking the drama out of the sport, turning it into an insipid vehicle for blue-chip advertising. Modern equipment is condemned, meanwhile, for reducing the game to an unsophisticated slug-fest and thus all but eliminating the need for finesse. The USGA and R&A are criticized for letting that happen.

Shackelford, an American, is talking primarily about the state of the game in the US, but figures for the number of people taking up golf in the UK, and many other countries in the world, are similarly stagnant.

Of course, many of the problems are the inevitable result of capitalism which, I'm guessing, most readers would like to keep. Green fees are as high as they are because enough people are willing to pay them. The same goes for our drivers, technological

masterpieces that are superseded just a few months after we buy them. Barring big changes in demographics and golfers' growing inclination to spend more time with their families, that's unlikely to change. What we must put a stop to right now, however, are the overuse of water and chemicals – fast-running courses are more exciting than lush dart-board courses – four- or five-hour rounds, and tedious 7,000-plus yard layouts with no personality (we don't enjoy them, so please don't build them).

As for clipping equipment's wings, I understand why many people want that to happen. But I'm surely not alone in hoping it doesn't, not for amateurs anyway. Perhaps bifurcation: one ball for tournament pros, one for the rest of us, is now a very real possibility, perhaps it is even a necessity?

No matter how good equipment gets though, most of the world's golfers will forever struggle. But in spite of that, or perhaps because of it, we'll always find a way to enjoy ourselves.

Oh well. Maybe some other round, another day.

INDEX

Aaron, Tommy 86
alignment 20

backspin 41, 74–5
bags 34
Ballesteros, Steve 23, 45, 52
ball(s)
    above feet 44
    angle of impact 22, 41, 74
    ball flight laws 28–9
    below feet 44
    choosing 16
    and course length 16–17
    positioning 22–3, 41, 74
    structure of 17
baseball grip 19
blade putters 15
blades 13
books 110
bosses, playing with 91
bounce (wedges) 14
break 55
breakfast 77
bunkers 31, 66–7

caddies 120–1
cart bags 34
cavity-back irons 12–13
celebrating, etiquette of 52
cheating 89
    and handicaps 118
children 45, 87
chip shots 64–5
clothing 42–3
    see also gloves; hats; shoes
clubs
    custom-fitted 84–5
    re-gripping 102
    suppliers 104–5
    see also drivers; hybrids;
    irons; putters; wedges

core strengthening
    exercises 76
course management 30–1
courses
    and the environment 82
    flowers on 65
    lengthening 16–17, 37
    links 46–7
    municipal 81
    off-piste 115
    ten favourite 51
    'uniqueness' of 45
crazy golf 69
crotch hooks 108
curving the ball 92–3

Daly, John 18, 75
dawn/dusk 51
De Vicenzo, Roberto 86
Demaret, Jimmy 42
distance-measuring devices
    96–7
downhill shots 44
    putts 31
drinks carts 59
drivers 10–11
driving ranges 58

Emotional Freedom Techniques
    (EFT) 98
environmental issues 82
etiquette
    basic rules 95
    for celebrating 52
    irritating habits 109
    19th hole 69
exercise
    for core strengthening 76
    golf as 105
    stretches 32–3

fades 93
Faldo, Nick 7, 75
focal dystonia 98
food and nutrition 59, 77

gamesmanship 71
Garcia, Sergio 111
gifts 119
gloves 35
golf trips 116–17
golfing gods 83
GPS units 96–7
grain 55
greens, reading 54–5
grip
    baseball 19
    interlocking 19
    for putting 40–1
    slices and 18, 60–1
    Vardon 19
    weak v. strong 18–19
grips, changing 102

handicaps 118–19
hats 97
heroes 45
Hogan, Ben 23, 42
hole in one 48–9
hooks 18, 28, 111
    intentional 92–3
hybrids 24

interlocking grip 19
irons 12–13

Jacobs, John 19, 28, 29
Jones, Bobby 7, 38
Jones, Ernest 26, 27

Kolezynski, Joe 122–3

Langer, Bernhard 18, 52, 98
laser rangefinders 96–7
lessons
    and couples 121
    pros 38–9
    unwanted advice 114
links 46–7
lob shots 80
loft
    drivers 11
    wedges 14

mallets 15
Masters tickets 56–7
matchplay 99
Mickelson, Phil 80
mirrors 112
Montgomerie, Colin 93
municipal courses 81
muscle-back irons 13

Nelson, Larry 87
nerves 25, 107
Nicklaus, Jack 15, 16, 20, 29,
    38, 42, 123
Norman, Greg 38, 97

online retailers/auctions 104–5
Open Championship 88
overlapping grip 19

Palmer, Arnold 16, 38, 42
Parnevik, Jesper 42–3
Penick, Harvey 18
photography 73
pitch marks, removing 95
pitch shots 53
Player, Gary 42
plumb-bobbing 54–5
positive affirmations 122–3

posture 21
power shots 76
pre-shot routine 94, 107
pro shops 104
pros 68
    picking 38–9
    pro-am matches 90
psychologists 122–3
putters 15
putting
    basic technique 40–1
    the good putter 70
    and grain 55
    at home 113
    plumb-bobbing 54–5
    practising 62–3
    reading the greens 54–5
    in strong wind 101
    uphill/downhill 31

rankings 51
rules 89

safety 95
St Andrews 16, 45, 124
Sanders, Doug 42
Sarazen, Gene 14
score keeping 86
scrambles 102
shafts, custom-fitted 85
shank, the 72
shoes 35
slices
    ball flight laws and 28
    fixes 60–1
    and grip 18, 60–1
    intentional 93
    and tee height 111
sloping lies 44
speeches 75

sports psychologists 112–13
strategy 30–1
stretching exercises 32–3
sun protection 57
suppliers 104–5
swing, the 26–7, 123

T-Rite 111
T-squares 108–9
tees 111
Texas scramble, the 102
tournaments
    Masters 56–7
    Open Championship 88
    scrambles 102
    on TV 59
training aids 108–9, 112–13
travel 83, 116–17
Twain, Mark 23

uphill shots 44
    putts 31

Vardon, Harry 98
Vardon grip 19

warm ups 36–7
water
    drinking 77
    as a hazard 106
Watson, Tom 38, 42, 52
wedges 14
weighted clubs 108–9
wind 100–1
Woods, Tiger 16, 23, 38, 43, 45,
    50, 97
Woosnam, Ian 93

yips, the 98

*TO SAM — LOOKING
FORWARD TO OUR FIRST
PROPER GAME TOGETHER.*

*A BIG THANK YOU TO
JEFF SHELLEY AND
DAVE CASTLEBERRY FOR
THEIR SUGGESTIONS AND
ENCOURAGEMENT.*